"Most rock memoirs are about excess. But Nic Brown's *Bang Bang Crash* is about ambivalence. It asks, What happens if you get everything you ever wanted and discover that you should have wanted something else? What should you do next? Well, in Nic Brown's case, he put down his drumsticks and wrote this charming, funny, rueful, wise book about the rock and roll life, and the life after the rock and roll life. An essential addition to the long, ongoing American story of second chances, second acts."

—Brock Clarke, author of *Who Are You, Calvin Bledsoe?*

BANG

    BANG

CRASH

ALSO BY NIC BROWN

Floodmarkers
Doubles: A Novel
In Every Way: A Novel

BANG

BANG

CRASH

A Memoir

Nic Brown

COUNTERPOINT
BERKELEY, CALIFORNIA

Bang Bang Crash

First Counterpoint edition: 2023

Library of Congress Cataloging-in-Publication Data
Names: Brown, Nic, 1977– author.
Title: Bang bang crash : a memoir / Nic Brown.
Description: First Counterpoint edition. | Berkeley : Counterpoint Press, 2023.
Identifiers: LCCN 2022038862 | ISBN 9781640094406 (trade paperback) | ISBN 9781640094413 (ebook)
Subjects: LCSH: Brown, Nic, 1977– | Drummers (Musicians)—United States—Biography. | Rock musicians—United States—Biography. | Authors, American—21st century—Biography. | LCGFT: Autobiographies.
Classification: LCC ML419.B763 A3 2023 | DDC 782.42166092 [B]—dc23/eng/20220816
LC record available at https://lccn.loc.gov/2022038862

Cover design by Lexi Earle
Book design by Laura Berry

COUNTERPOINT
2560 Ninth Street, Suite 318
Berkeley, CA 94710
www.counterpointpress.com

Printed in the United States of America

10 9 8 7 6 5 4 3 2 1

For Mark

CONTENTS

BANG

BANG

CRASH

PROLOGUE | DRUMMING

Let's say it comes up at a dinner party. We're at a friend's house and the food is moving around the table. There's potato salad. Cheap beer. It's a potluck. Everything is very relaxed. Someone is talking about their son who is learning to play the drums.

"Oh, Nic was in a band," someone says.

A few heads turn. Most people here know me, but a few don't.

"Well, a lot of bands, actually," I say, as if to fracture their focus. I take the pasta. It's clear I'm trying to move away from the subject. "But yeah, I used to play the drums."

"No no, but what's the band?" they say. Then to the table, "Nic had a hit song."

The mood changes at this, like an interesting and unexpected animal has just entered the room. Fascinating and exciting to some, uncomfortable and out of place to me.

"Well," I say. "Yeah. But there are a lot of hit songs. And it wasn't a big hit."

"Wait, what was it?" somebody says, someone who doesn't know me. "Do I know it?"

I tell them they don't. That there are twenty different charts with twenty different top twenty songs today, right now, at this very moment, and likely none of us know number twenty on any of them. Or fourteen. That's what we got to, I think, on *Billboard*'s alternative rock chart in the summer of 1998. It was many years ago now. I name the song, the band. Maybe I mention a few other groups that I played with. They don't know any of them. Most people don't anymore. I tell them that my first record deal was with a band that I formed to play my eighth-grade dance. That right after high school we signed a contract with Atlantic Records. That I did that for a few years and then moved on to play with other acts, some bigger, some better, before finally calling it quits.

"Well, I'll have to look you up," they say.

I make a joke about the internet. That things are maybe better left in the nineties. Because if they do look me up, they won't recognize anything that I did. I was like a baseball player who gets called up for a few seasons on a subpar team. I made it to the majors, but you don't remember me. I wasn't one of the greats. I was just good enough.

I reach for the bread. The conversation moves on. The topic of my past as a musician lingers, though, like a mist. It clouds my vision for a while—maybe even until I get home that night, trailing vapors of it into the bed with me.

Elizabeth Bishop said once that there's nothing more embarrassing than being a poet. To which I thought, when I read it: try being a drummer. How can you tell if the stage is level? The drummer is drooling out of both sides of his mouth. What's the last thing a drummer says to his band? Let's try one of my songs. Who's the guy who always hangs around with musicians? A drummer. My profession is a literal punch line. As a child the dream of drumming was gilded with romance and the promise of thrill. As an adult, though, I have learned, your childhood dream can become something else entirely, especially if it comes true.

At the grocery store in Greensboro, sometimes I see people I knew growing up.

"Nic! Still playing the drums?" they'll say, dropping a box of cereal into their cart.

"Not really," I say.

"No?"

We move out of the way of someone passing by, talk about our children. Sometimes I feel bad for having said that I don't still play, as if I'm letting these people down.

"Well, I do teach my daughter sometimes," I might add.

But the truth is I never do play the drums. That's only if I'm talking about hitting a drum with a stick, though. The real answer, the one that is more accurate, is that I am always playing the drums. That rhythms and songs and patterns are dancing constantly through my mind, twirling in and around the beat of the windshield wipers, the thud of my footsteps, or the click of my grocery cart as I wheel it away.

Every day and everywhere I go I tap complicated patterns out on my teeth. I've done this for years. Am doing it right now, as I type. Each cusp is a different tone. The side of a molar on my upper right is the hi-hat cymbal. The bass drum is just a tooth back. My snare is a touch of the bottom incisors against the back of the top ones. Fills happen by sliding my jaw to the left and the right, clicking my teeth together in a quick succession of eighth notes like I'm gently swishing wine. The sound is incredible inside my head: resonant, deep, and totally mine.

"You must grind your teeth," the dentist keeps saying, as he prods deeply into my mouth. "Do you grind your teeth?"

"No," I say, with difficulty, as he squeaks a latex-covered thumb on a molar.

"You have serious wear patterns," he says. This happens every time I go to him. He digs his metal poker into an actual pit that has opened up in one tooth on my bottom left side. "Your wife ever say you grind your teeth at night?"

"No."

He keeps prodding as I stare into the light.

I can't bring myself to explain to him what it is that I've done. That I've tapped actual holes into my teeth. That I play them like a secret drum set inside my mouth. Part of me is afraid the dentist will think I am crazy. Another part is afraid that he'll tell me to stop.

"What song are you playing right now?" my wife, Abby, says, eyeing my thighs as I twitch along to a tune heard only inside my head. I'm playing along with my teeth too, but that she can't see.

"Oh." I stop the tapping and flexing. I didn't even know I was doing it. It takes me a second to identify the melody, as if

I must consult a separate person within me who is almost too busy to answer.

How do other people listen to the world? Do they carefully note that the chorus of this Dua Lipa song playing on 98.1 FM right now has just started with an utterly unexpected accent on the four instead of the downbeat? When no one is looking, do they play air shaker to the sixteenth notes on the bridge? When they go jogging, do they inhale one quarter note and two shorter eighth notes on the first two steps, then exhale two woofing half notes on the following ones, every time, with every sequence of steps that they take, for miles and miles and miles?

I never play the drums anymore, but they never cease playing me.

I'm no longer a drummer. But still, always, I'm drumming.

1 | HOW TO ACHIEVE SUCCESS IN THE NORTH CAROLINA MUSIC SCENE IN THE YEARS BETWEEN 1990 AND 1997

First you eat the dried seaweed that Ken Tanaka's mother gives you, placing each thin sheet onto your palm with a pair of chrome tongs, and then you go to the playroom. You're already too old to call it a playroom—you're in eighth grade—but still, you call it the playroom. There's a silver oyster Slingerland drum set from the sixties in there, one that you would kill for now but at the time seems a bit cheap and weird, and while you can play that drum set well—you've been taking lessons from Pete Crawford for four years already—you don't necessarily want to play Ken's drums just for the sake of playing his drums. Today, though, Ken's friend Mark Kano is in the playroom too, and he has a guitar. Mark is a few years older and half Korean and has dark shaggy hair and seems unassuming and will not be the first person with whom you've played. Already you will have been in the Punktuals for several months, a band whose members are all a bit older than you—you met them at UNCG band camp—and who perform Ramones covers almost exclusively, except for that one time when you told them you also really liked "Magic Carpet Ride" by Steppenwolf and they all got sort of quiet and awkward for a moment before finally agreeing to run through it. But Mark can sing much better than the singer of the Punktuals, a young man who produces little more than a yelp, and Mark is singing "Hotel California," and his voice is better than any voice you've ever been in the same room with before and so you play along. In the corner by the karaoke machine, Ken slips in a cassette. He presses record. Afterward when he plays the tape back for you, everyone in the playroom will be shocked, because what it sounds like is not two kids fooling around. What it sounds like is a song.

You play the eighth-grade dance.
You play the battle of the bands and come in third.
You play Mike Biser's backyard party and take off your shirt.
You play the bonfire and the pep rally, twice.

You make your own T-shirts by spray-painting the name Athenaeum onto them using a stencil. Athenaeum is the name your mother has suggested for your band, a name which to your ears sounds a bit like Dionysus, the local high school band you idolize, so you decide it will work. Even though no one can say it or spell it.

You use the high school Xerox machine to photocopy the famous Richard Avedon photo of an alopecic half-naked man covered in bees and then write the word ATHENAEUM in the white space above him. Below you draw a small map leading to the farm of Timothy Bell, the guy now playing guitar with you and Mark. PARTY, the flyer announces, and to this party people do come. Lots of people. Hundreds maybe. In the pasture a stage has been built in the days leading up to the show, constructed by a group of high schoolers from Page, all of whom are older than you—you are always the youngest—and on this stage, during the very last song, Timothy slams down his guitar, kneels over it, and lights it on fire. Only the guitar is not a real guitar. It is a fake guitar, made to look like a red Gibson SG, an object that Timothy has constructed from scrap wood and cardboard in his basement for the sole purpose of burning at this very moment. At first, though, the guitar won't catch fire, so Timothy has to squirt some lighter fluid onto it, and even then the flames are so small you're not sure anyone can see them. The crowd is confused. You turn your face away and feel glad to have drums behind which you can hide.

You play Kilroy's.
You play the Blind Tiger.
You play Kilroy's again but now it is called the Zoo Bar.

You spend hours in the attic with Mark, who can already drive, so sometimes when you get home from school his red Nissan pickup truck is already parked at the curb. Inside, his baby sister will be sitting on the chopping block with your mother, who will say hi, and then you will rush upstairs to find Mark working on a song called "Summertime." Or you will find him working on a song called "Haircut." Or you will find him working on a song called "On My Mind," a song that after you play it with him for the first time fills you with such amazement that later you lay on your bed imagining just what it means about your life to have been involved in its creation.

You drive around the neighborhood with Mark in his red Nissan, listening to demos of your new songs only minutes after recording them. You are silent, more alert to what you are hearing than you will be to any sound ever again. You cannot wait to play what you have created for your girlfriend. For your brother. For your friend Bryce, who has the best taste. You feel like you have just found a new planet. That you have discovered a lifesaving device. That the future has been revealed to you and Mark, but no one else knows it yet. The secret is only there with you inside Mark's truck. You feel you need to scream. Sometimes you scream.

You listen to Toad the Wet Sprocket, a lot. You listen to Matthew Sweet. The Lemonheads. Dillon Fence. The Sex Police. They Might Be Giants. Beastie Boys and the Connells and that first Violent Femmes record. You have an Enya tape that you play frequently for several weeks until Bryce's roommate at the School of the Arts hears you playing it and says, "Ah, he likes the Enya," and then you cease listening to it, realizing that Enya is embarrassing. You have a tape by Yo La Tengo, a band who is undeniably cool, but you don't know that yet. You just know that the guy at Spins received it as part of a promotional package and was going to throw it away but then you came in and he gave it to you instead. At night, after the lights have been turned off, you listen to that Yo La Tengo tape on your headphones. It's autumnal, the sound of that record, and it's actually the autumn of your fifteenth year when you are listening to it, and so somehow this makes you feel nostalgic for autumns of years long past, but how can you even feel that way when you're only fifteen? You do, though. When you listen to this album again at age forty-three, you will experience a different type of nostalgia, one for days that you actually did live through, the very days being described here, days when every second seems to be spent thinking of music. And how great is it that you get to make that music with Mark? Because Mark is, why not admit it, so much more talented than you are. He has a gift so great as to be almost a burden to him. He hears things you cannot—that harmony is off, oh, the compression is too much, I need to adjust my new chorus pedal et cetera, et cetera—and these things that he hears complicate his life much more than your life is complicated. Because you're just the drummer. And you don't hear much more than the drums, to be honest. But in a way that's a blessing, and whatever you bring to the equation seems to add value. Something about your connection makes it all possible. And Mark has also become your closest friend, something you can now look back on and see clearly, but at the time you would never acknowledge, because already you and Mark treat each other like something beyond merely friends. Friends hang out and have fun. You two, though—it's a type of human alchemy. You create magic from nothing, just pulling sound from the air.

You record a cassette and walk around Ross Van der Linden's backyard during a party at the end of the '94 school year, selling copies out of a blue L.L.Bean duffle bag. You record a new batch of songs in a studio inside a small house in Raleigh over the summer and print them up on CDs, selling copies at shows, copies that suddenly seem to be everywhere. You pull up to a stoplight at the intersection of Aycock and Benjamin Parkway one afternoon and hear your own song coming in through the window. When you look over and find Mr. Zimmerman there in the car beside you—he's the new history teacher, the one who played basketball at Davidson and is only twenty-two and who all the high school girls have a crush on—you are shocked. He doesn't even seem to be embarrassed, though. "Sounds good!" he says, and gives a thumbs-up.

You will say yes when the manager of the Schoolkids in Raleigh asks to be your manager. You will drive to that Schoolkids and stand against many brick walls while a photographer tries to find just the right one, until finally the brick wall inside the bathroom is determined to be the best brick wall for the photo, and so you stand shoulder to shoulder in the Schoolkids bathroom and have your first promo shots taken.

Mark graduates from Smith, said to be one of the worst high schools in the city. He finds work as a cook at Garden Café on Battleground, next to Blockbuster, where he makes a ginger dressing so excellent that you all joke about bottling the stuff and selling it in grocery stores. There are no real plans for Mark to sell bottled dressing, though. Or to cook. His only goal is music. You are still in high school, however, attending Greensboro Day School, the best private school in the city, and everyone there applies to college and so you apply too. You're a good student. You love books. Already you love writing. Nonetheless, your acceptance letters come as a shock. Perhaps the fact that you are in a semi-successful band already has helped, but still, when you get into Princeton it feels like a big deal. And Columbia lets you in too. And Duke, a school that offers you a three-quarters scholarship because of an essay you wrote on the assigned topic of "peer leadership" in which you recounted the time Bryce made a home movie called *Flesh Eating Skate Zombies from Hell*. It all seems hard to believe. Perhaps these schools have only accepted you because they can smell your indifference. Perhaps part of your appeal is that they know you might not even want to attend them in the first place. That you already have so much going on with Mark, so much you are passionate about without them, that you might just say no to them all. And even when the director of the jazz band at Princeton calls one afternoon with the pitch that you could play there too, you think you can hear in his voice an understanding that he knows just as well as you do that you shouldn't actually come to play drums with the jazz band at Princeton, because obviously what you should do is keep playing with Mark.

So you keep playing with Mark. You do not go to Princeton. Or Columbia. Or Duke. You do not go to any college at all. What you do is take a job as a carpenter's assistant with a man named Matthew Butwinski and move into a crummy rental house with three roommates. There are whispers, perhaps among parents of classmates, that you have thrown away all potential. Success is at hand, though. You think it is, at least. You dream of it.

You awake at 6:00 a.m. and caulk the trim at Barrington Place. You back prime the soffits. You clean the gutters at the house of Maddie Robinson's parents who are shocked to find you—Nic Brown, from Greensboro Day School?—on the top of a ladder. You grow so conditioned to the rank stink of the landfill that, before you even reach it with that day's trailer of scraps, you gag just by reflex. This is only your daylight activity, though. After dark is when you drive to Amos' in Charlotte and open for Jolene, when you play the Skylight Exchange in Chapel Hill with John Gillespie, when you do an industry showcase in Wilmington at the Mad Monk and play a bar in Florence for no one but the bartender and his dog. This is what keeps you immune from despair. It is your inoculation of hope.

Your manager has "gotten a call from RCA." Your manager has "gotten a call from someone at Capitol." Your manager has "gotten a call from Interscope." It will happen! It's happening! You tell your mother and your girlfriend and Bryce. You tell everyone. But then it doesn't happen, and you are embarrassed, and quickly learn to resist all excitement, tucking your dreams away into some type of cocoon where you guard them, carefully, keeping them safe.

After watching Alanis Morissette perform on a televised awards show, you become overcome with emotion. Because of Alanis

Morissette! You don't even like her. She is just someone on the radio. But seeing her on this television show makes you feel an envy that is somehow amplified to an unbearable level because of what can only be described as a closeness you feel to Alanis Morissette, as if the television is not an electrified box but rather a window that you are just on the other side of. That you can almost step through and be on that stage in place of her, performing for all those people. Your band is as good. With just a few things going your way, you can see how it could happen. But the fact that it has not happened makes you drive your red Karmann Ghia to Fisher Park, where you stop beneath a giant oak tree along the bank of Buffalo Creek and sit there in a heavy thrumming silence, feeling as if some mysterious force is expanding within you and about to pop out, at which point you will surely punch your dashboard or scream or bang your head on the steering wheel. None of which you do, because there are people around, but all of which you feel.

Maybe the part that matters least is when it does happen. When you actually do sign a six-album record deal with Atlantic Records, which will indeed take place inside an office in Manhattan on an afternoon in 1997. But already you will feel cold by then. It will not be the success you had dreamed of, even though it is exactly the success you had dreamed of. The peak will have already been reached, somehow, and nothing will ever again feel as pure.

So back up from that day in Manhattan, go back step by step, and look for the moment. When you could tell someone in all seriousness that your dreams had just come true. When everything you'd longed for felt like it had just been attained. When somehow it all felt the best.

There it is. It's in Raleigh in 1996.

You're in a filthy house on a busted couch. Mark is there too, and Grey, the handsome soccer player from Charlotte who plays guitar with you now. You're backstage, which isn't behind any stage. It's just some guy's bedroom. This is only a house, after all, not a real club, it's just a college party at NC State. You're cold, bored. Maybe staring at the wall while Mark makes some set lists. And then Alex comes in. He is your bass player, an almost too-intelligent young man with red hair and a kind face who drives a '93 Mustang, and as soon as he enters the room you know he has news. There are a couple college guys there with you, people you don't know, and Alex says, "Give us a second?" Probably these young men live in the house. This could be their own bedroom. Still, they leave it, and before the door closes behind them, you feel as if Alex could tell you anything. That he could deliver news of an alien life-form. That you've all won the lottery. That human flight is suddenly possible. You live in just such a state of heightened expectation during these days, waiting for news of transformation. What you really want Alex to say, though, is that a label is making an offer.

He says it.

You don't scream. You don't jump around. You soak it up silently. And it isn't even a record deal. It's just a publishing deal, for now. But it's from EMI, and you can see in your mind the EMI logo on the covers of your Beatles albums, especially *Revolver*, your favorite. And now they want to sign you.

For some reason you cannot recall, Alex explains that the news must remain secret for the time being, and surprisingly you all keep it that way. You do not tell any of the people who are pouring into the house for your show, a state of affairs that, over the next few hours, will serve to make the news feel all the more potent. Watching a roomful of sweaty students dance around you at the end of the night, you feel a strange power over them, telling yourself that you will never play another college party like this again. That they have no idea what all you're getting ready to do.

The next morning is icy, just after sunrise. The sky is overcast and gray. You have not slept much. Overnight, the knowledge has seeped into you like a dye, spreading, changing everything it touches. You're in the Nissan with Mark, both of you silent as you drive west on I-40. His truck is drafty and cold and the windows are clouded with thick condensation. Beside you, you rub one small spot clear on the glass. You will remember this feeling forever, of watching the highway flash by through that spot, moving from blur to sharp focus to blur. You imagine as you watch it what the owner of Spins will think when he learns. What Bryce might say. How a few of the girls from high school

will react. And then that will be it, that morning, on the drive
back to Greensboro. That's when you feel you've achieved all
you wanted.

By the time you get home, it will be over. The phone calls
will have already begun. Negotiations about advance amounts
and who will get what. This will go on for weeks. Months.
Years even, stretching past the point in the future when you
will do what seems only inevitable now, but at the time would
have felt nothing short of impossible, which is that you will quit
this band, you will bad-mouth its music, you will pretend to
have been too cool for it all along, even dismissing the songs—
the very songs you had loved so much that they felt like drugs
running through your veins—with statements like "they're just
pop songs." But that's all in the future. You're not there yet. Not
yet not yet not yet. For now, you're not even home. You're just
rolling west on I-40 with Mark, the happiest you'll be in your
life, with the world all around you shrouded in fog except for
that one tiny spot.

2 | PETE

I'm deep in the crowd as the band comes onstage. A cheer swells up around me as I rise to my toes, but just as I do the roar starts to fade. I peer over heads, pushing, struggling to see what is wrong—then all at once it becomes clear. There's a vacancy at the back of the stage. Ringo, it seems, isn't there.

"I'm sorry," John says, stepping up to the mic. "But Ringo is sick. Does anyone here play the drums?"

It's like a dream come true, I think, as I raise my hand in the air. But of course it isn't a dream come true. It's really just a dream that's a dream, because I'm not at a Beatles concert at all. I'm twelve years old and asleep in my bed. Still, it's thrilling as John calls me onstage.

"You know the songs?" he says.

"Oh yeah," I say.

But what I think is: John, you have no idea. I've played along with every Beatles song ever recorded while wearing my tiny Sony headphones plugged into the black boombox propped on the tall green stool beside my drum set in my mother's attic.

So when I sit down behind Ringo's Ludwigs and count us into "Come Together," I nail every note. This scene played out often during the nights of my childhood. It was the only recurring dream I ever had. But I had another dream too, one that filled my waking hours for years: the dream of being a drummer. Of making a living from it, of doing it for real. And for a while this dream became a reality, and for a long time it was spectacular. But what I'm asking now is what happens to your childhood dream once you grow up? What happens when you discover that you're a grown man, living out the dreams of a boy?

"He's just so embarrassed," my friend Matthew tells an acquaintance after the topic of my music career comes up and I grow visibly uncomfortable, looking down in silence, telling myself it will pass.

"You have to own it," my father-in-law says. He likes to text me short videos of himself singing along to the one radio hit that I played on. It brings him great pleasure to imagine the discomfort this brings me.

"You do act incredibly weird about it," my friend Brandon says, a man who plays the guitar and sings in his living room with such effortless joy that it feels like a reproach. "I mean, if I could do one thing as well as you play the drums, I would talk about it all the time."

But I do not talk about it all the time. In fact, for the most part, I don't speak of it at all. Most people in my life—coworkers, students, neighbors, new friends—don't even know that I play a musical instrument, let alone that I once had a successful career doing so. And if it does come up in conversation, there have been times when I have literally felt ill afterward, groaning aloud when replaying the exchange in my mind. I make a dramatic promise to myself in these moments, telling myself that I will never speak of it again.

Yet here I am, speaking of it. Trying to figure out what my problem is, because, in truth, I've never been able to explain exactly what it is that so troubles me about discussing my life as a musician. There was no scandalous downfall. I was not kicked out of any band for idiotic behavior. I never even went to an audition that I didn't get. I simply had a dream and I followed it, then left it behind.

"You should be proud!" a student says, watching my face grow red at the mention of my drumming. But what she doesn't get is that I am proud. It's just that there are things complicating my pride. Things I have a hard time explaining even to myself. So, like the ghost of music past, I'm taking us back to a time before embarrassment. To the headwaters of joy. Because if I can trace its course from there, perhaps I can find where the waters grow murky.

I guess this all leads back to Pete.

It's 1986. I am eight. I suppose I'm nervous. My mother, a petite forty-one-year-old with chic cropped hair and sinewy limbs, is behind the wheel of our hunter green S108 Mercedes sedan. This is in Greensboro, North Carolina, and we have just backed out of our driveway and are heading east on Country Club Drive. The golf course runs beside us on the right. On the left is the house where that postmaster general who was appointed by Trump now lives, along with his wife, the former ambassador to Estonia, and then beside them is a house with its own tennis court—and adjoining *tennis court house*—and then next to that is a white columned mansion where candidates for the Republican presidential nomination always seem to be showing up for fundraisers. I don't personally know the people who live in these houses today, but back then, when I was eight, I knew the families inside them. Their kids went to school with me. I lived one block away. This was my world. And soon another part of my world, the Greensboro Country Club, appears on our right, with its tennis courts and pool and exclusive all-white membership.

We turn right onto Elm Street and in less than a mile are downtown, driving through the negative image of Country Club Drive. Here there might as well be tumbleweeds. The elegant old buildings, like the 1930 art deco Kress and the Jefferson Standard (built in 1923, when it was the tallest building in North Carolina), are all empty or seem like they should to be. Windows are taped up. Through one you can see a desolate showroom filled with nothing but an old sink and a ladder, wires dangling from the ceiling above.

We pass Woolworth's, home to the lunch counter where, in 1960, four students from nearby NC A&T University enacted one of the first sit-ins of the civil rights movement. And though it is 1986 on this day as my mother and I drive past, it was only seven years earlier and a handful of blocks away that a group of marching Klansmen and American Nazi Party members got into a gunfight with protesters that left five people dead.

This is not to say that my mother and I feel any sense of danger as we turn onto Market Street. At least not that I am aware of. My mother seems completely at ease as she parks in front of a small industrial storefront whose sign reads Harvey West Music.

Inside, she speaks to a friendly older man behind the

counter. Another man is there too, leaning on the railing: a quiet middle-aged Black man wearing wire-rim glasses. The lenses are darkened, but behind them, one eye is milky and mysterious, its pupil a cloudy enigma. The other one, though—the good eye—is trained right on me.

This is Pete. And he's about to give me my first drum lesson.

It might help sharpen the focus here if I describe what I'm wearing. I cannot remember the exact outfit, but I will pick a representative selection from my wardrobe of the time. I have on a large "beret" made by the surf wear company Jimmy'z, a hat that is basically just a droopy oversized cloth bag with bright yellow stripes held on to my head by a white Velcro strap. I wear a dark blue Per Welinder Powell-Peralta skateboarding shirt, a shirt that celebrates the world's second-best freestyle skateboarder with a skull in a Viking helmet holding a sword in front of his face. I wear this shirt backward so that the large image is front and center on my chest, making the collar ride a touch high on my neck. I wear a different colored argyle sock on each foot, and mismatched Converse high-tops. I am a little bit pudgy, and my hair is shaved short everywhere except for my bangs, which hang out of my beret at such length that, if they do not reach my chin already, they will soon.

So this is the boy Pete is looking at through his tinted glasses, the boy who he then invites to follow him into the back, where we enter a small practice space in which I see no drums, only an upright piano and some old cardboard boxes.

"Don't keep your index fingers extended," he says, as he adjusts a pair of drumsticks in my hands. "Don't hold the sticks too tightly. Keep your pinky in. There you go."

He nudges one of the boxes in front of me—it is to be my drum, I understand—and proceeds to teach me how to para-diddle on it. Paradiddles are one of the "rudiments," drum-ming's foundational exercises, and the sticking pattern—right left right right, left right left left—is something I struggle with that day but can now tap without even thinking, in the same way I imagine some people might unconsciously count a rosary.

"How was it?" my mother asks when I emerge.

"Fine?" I say.

The lesson is only a whim. If the next one is bad I'll just quit. I've done the same with karate and horseback riding before.

I must have known already, though, before the memory had time to fade, that this would be a turning point in my life. Because why else would I remember the contours of Harvey West's dim interior, punctuated by the flash of chrome and brass? The horns, catching light on the rims. The stand-up bass, the Fender Rhodes. And the drums: those sparkle-finish old Lud-wigs stacked atop one another. Grimy Zildjians for sale, some even cracked. Drumsticks like miniature baseball bats sorted into cubbyholes marked for different sizes.

Maybe I'm making this up. Maybe this isn't what Harvey West looked like that day, or maybe this is what it looked like on another day, much later. It's hard to tell. That store closed long ago. Maybe Pete didn't even teach me how to paradiddle that day. I don't know. What matters, though, is that I'm still tapping out those strokes that he taught me, right now, right here on my desktop. Right left right right left right left left and so on like some incessant message being sent out from deep in my past.

The following year is fifth grade, and for the first time band is offered at school. Entering the classroom on our first day, the air is filled with the sound of students honking through newly purchased horns. I feel like a long-distance runner placed in a roomful of toddlers, not because of any innate talent on my part, but simply because I have continued to take lessons from Pete over the past year, and so compared to my classmates, many of whom have never played a note, I am light years ahead.

"Hey what's your favorite beat?" someone says, when they learn I can play.

"I don't have a favorite beat," I say.

The question seems stupid to me even then, because already I understand that a drum pattern is never as appealing on its own as it is when it's part of a song.

My classmates are undeterred, though. They ask if I can play various songs off the radio, naming this one or that one, but not only do I not know the parts for these songs, I don't know the names of these songs. This is because Pete has— already, gently, obliquely, like a skipper steering a boat through a current—been guiding my tastes. And Pete disdains popular music. Rock and roll, especially very popular rock and roll, is the worst. What Pete prefers is jazz, and so I've found that I too now listen to jazz, spinning Dizzy Gillespie and John Coltrane and Miles Davis and Thelonious Monk and Louis Armstrong and Duke Ellington alone in my bedroom. And while I am into the Beatles as well, and Pete thinks the Beatles are fine, he's also made it clear that rock and roll is not worth thinking too much about musically. Jazz is the ultimate goal.

My classmates don't want to hear jazz, though. They want "Pour Some Sugar on Me" or "Bust a Move" or "Livin' on a Prayer" or "Walk This Way." None of which I know. So I play the only rock part of interest that I can think of, which is Ringo's "solo" off "The End" from *Abbey Road*. It's just a syncopated little pattern over a four-on-the-floor bass drum thud, but as I play it my classmates grow quiet. It's like I've cast a spell.

"What was that?" they say when I finish.

"That was . . . Ringo," I say.

And then they tell me to do it again.

It's a demand that only increases in frequency over the next several weeks. "Ringo, Ringo," my classmates chant at the start of each class, "Ringo, Ringo," until eventually the teacher has to start telling me to just play the damn thing before she can begin, because it's the only way to get the room quiet.

Instead of reveling in the attention, though, already I find the situation a little embarrassing. Ringo's drum part, after all, is simple and technically easy—even a bit silly, in my opinion—so my classmates' obsession with it seems somehow disappointing. Shouldn't they want something better? Something more impressive? More troubling than even these concerns, though, is the persistent feeling that if Pete were to hear me playing it—and see these classmates cheering as I did so—he would somehow be disappointed.

Lessons with Pete move out of Harvey West and into the third-floor playroom of my five-bedroom, 5,100-square-foot white brick house on Country Club Drive. He comes once a week in an old blue Volvo wagon that he parks at the curb, not far from the bus stop where the neighborhood maids—all Black women in starched white clothing—arrive in the mornings.

Upstairs, settling into a creaky armchair, Pete sips from an IBC root beer that my mother has given him. "Play for me," he says, and I run lines from a book called *Stick Control*. I run lines from a book called *Advanced Techniques for the Modern Drummer*. I run lines from a book called *Progressive Steps to Syncopation for the Modern Drummer*. I play a bossa nova. I play a seven-stroke roll. I ride left-handed.

If something sounds right, Pete might nod. Usually, though, he just picks up on a technical problem and works with me to correct it. Sometimes, if I cannot get it right, he will stand behind me and extend his arms, wrapping his large hands over my own tiny ones—drumsticks still in my grasp—and play the part himself. It is there, within Pete's embrace, that I can play the impossible.

During this time, my father lives in Switzerland. He and my mother divorced a year or two back, but before that he traveled often. Or maybe he was just at the office all the time. Maybe both. I'm not sure. I was young. The point is I don't have too many memories of him being in the house even when he was in it, so by the time he moves out, his absence doesn't feel like much of an absence at all. It is an uncomplication in our relationship, which, if distant because of actual distance, has always been otherwise very good. Still, I am a human child, one with a mother now raising two boys alone while working as a tax accountant, one whose brother has an obsessive fixation on annoying sounds—especially the many annoying sounds made by a little brother incessantly drumming—and so when I find myself alone in my bedroom, trying to be as quiet as possible so as not to annoy anyone, I do not lie beneath the plastic Swiss alps gondola that is strung from one side of the room to the other and dream only of riding in it with my father. What I do is lay there listening to John Coltrane's "My Favorite Things" on my headphones, memorizing the solos, playing along silently in hopes of making Pete proud.

In light of all this, it's easy to cast Pete as a father figure. I never picture Pete as a father, though. At all times he maintains a sphinx-like remove. He shares nothing with me about his life. I never know if he has children of his own, if he is married, what his age is, or where it is that he lives. He is always that thing perhaps even more important to me than a father: He is my teacher. Still, if there is one man whose approval I desire, it is Pete. And by the time I am thirteen, I have reason to start to believe that I've earned it.

This is when he starts to take me with him to gigs. Did I know the names of those clubs back then? If I did, I can't remember them now. It's almost like they don't exist in any real life, just that dreamworld with Pete. They are downtown in Greensboro, though, and inside them sit couples—both Black and white—at small tables in the dim light.

From my own little table I watch as Pete performs with a trio. I take in how his foot dances on the hi-hat pedal—the heel lifting at times, at others staying down. How he drinks water between songs. Where he puts the glass so it won't be in the way. How he crams one extra drumstick into the bass drum lug. How effortlessly he switches between brushes and sticks in the midst of a song. And then at last Pete gestures for me to come. This is what I've been waiting for. The drop in my stomach. The band makes no grand announcement. They simply prepare the next song as Pete stands up and I take his place.

"You know 'Mr. PC'?" the piano player might ask, glancing over his shoulder.

"Yeah, sure," I say.

"OK. Count us in."

Ding ding da-ding ding da-ding ding da-ding. You know the part. A dotted eighth sixteenth with the hi-hat chink on two and four. That's all I'm trying to do. To hang on for dear life. Maybe I flub a note here or there, but mostly I do fine, though once a bass player does snap at me for dragging during his solo.

"Don't play slow just cause you're playing quieter!" he whispers harshly, soloing high on the neck. "Quiet doesn't mean slow. Pick it up. OK, not that much. There you go."

I am proud to receive this bass player's rebuke, though, because even if I am dragging, I am doing it on Pete's drums, in a real nightclub that he has brought me to. My dream about filling in for Ringo has always been a satisfying fantasy, but this—sitting in for the actual living man whom I aspire to impress more than any other—is something much better.

When I meet Mark at Ken's house, the guitar he's playing is a semi-stolen classical model just recently strung with heavy acoustic guitar strings (strings that are slowly but inexorably pulling the bridge off the instrument's body, an inevitability only a month or so in its future, though of course we don't know this yet), and he can play a bunch of Eagles songs on that guitar and even better he can sing them in a deep voice as close to perfect as any voice I've ever been in the same room with before. So I play along, just loud enough to still be able to hear his guitar and his voice. This is not an easy thing to do—to play at the right volume, to not overwhelm, to accompany and not clobber—but it is what Pete has taught me. It's what I learned at all those gigs. Here, though, with Mark, I play without fear of rushing during anyone's bass solo. In fact, I have no fear at all, I'm just playing music with a friend of a friend, and so when we discover that we sound good together—almost like a real band, even though it's just the two of us—it comes as a total surprise. It is like we've uncovered some object of great worth hidden there in Ken's playroom, one we weren't even looking for. When I go home, though, the treasure is gone. It can exist only when Mark and I are together.

Pete forms a jazz group made up of his students. We call ourselves For Pete's Sake, a name that appears to bring Pete both embarrassment and a measure of restrained pleasure. (Eventually, after his suggestion, we will change the name to Percussion Discussion.) Everyone in the band is either from my neighborhood or my private school or both, which means we are all well-off and white, and while each member plays drums, most know another instrument too—piano, vibes, bass— meaning that between us there are enough melodic options to flesh out some standards. For Pete's Sake rehearsals now take the place of most of our individual lessons.

During what private lessons I still do have, though, I rarely play. These hours have become what I call "talking lessons." During talking lessons, Pete sits in my attic under a painting of Snoopy that my mother made on the wall years ago and tells me the story of his blind eye. How he became sick as a child and the only doctor in Greensboro who could treat him would not do so because he was Black. He tells me about how unusual it is for him, as a Black man, to be invited into our house on Country Club Drive. How my mother has done something important by asking him here. He tells me about the connections between mathematics and music. He tells me about his close friend, the drummer Dannie Richmond, who played almost his whole career with Charles Mingus. He talks about Dannie's struggles with drugs. Pete tells me about how, when he was young, his family didn't have a refrigerator, that they actually waited for an iceman to bring them a large piece of ice that Pete would then stow carefully within a metal-lined box. He tells me so many things like this during our talking lessons, stories that stay with me still, their details sharp and mysterious. None of these stories involve me playing music, though.

"Why don't we play drums anymore?" I say one afternoon. I deliver this question lightly, though, almost as a joke, because I don't really feel the situation is strange. Somehow it all seems to make sense. Still, Pete's reply is utterly serious.

"Because what I've taught you about the drums is only the alphabet," he says. "And now I have to teach you what to say with it."

It occurs to me now that I might not be writing only about my dreams here, but perhaps about Pete's dreams as well. Because at the time, Pete speaks with great satisfaction to us—the members of For Pete's Sake—about all the other local musicians who are befuddled by hearing us play. The subtext here is that Pete's students are amazing because (1) we can play (meaning we can *solo*, and have *feel* while doing so, and not be uptight semi-academic robots like so many other local jazz students), and (2) most importantly, we are the children of rich, white, Greensboro privilege. And yet we are his. And yet, we are playing *jazz*. This is not to suggest that we have been crafted into some type of cultural ambassadors by Pete, carrying with us a message of racial harmony through music. It is never that simple nor that explicit. All we are doing is playing music, and yet we are doing it with an understanding—an awareness cultivated by Pete—that by doing so, we are involved in something much larger than just making music. After all, we are the children of the doctor who would not treat Pete's eye. We are the children of the Klansmen who killed five people downtown in 1979. We are the children of the Woolworth's owners who refused to serve the Greensboro Four. And now we are the members of a band named For Pete's Sake. Something transgressive and important and vital is mixed into this dynamic, something huge and significant, and even if it is something we don't exactly define, we know it is there and that it is at the root of all that we love about being with Pete. And I think Pete feels it too, maybe more than any of us.

Or maybe not. I can't speak for him. Maybe none of this was in Pete's head. Perhaps he just wanted to find a way to keep his students busy once we reached competence on our instruments. For all I know, Pete doesn't even remember me, or any of us, or any of these events. I was only a boy, and he was my teacher.

He had many other students and a life outside it that I know nothing about. All I can say is that these are the things I felt at the time, and that because of them, drumming became much more important to me than the mere act of making music with drums.

Athenaeum, the band Mark and I form, is soon joined by a rotating cast of other musicians—local high school guitarists and bassists like Jamie and Bryan and Cullen and Alex—and though the identity of these people may change over time, the idea that Mark and I are at the center of a band has now stuck. Unlike For Pete's Sake—which plays standards written years before by Duke Ellington and John Coltrane and Miles Davis—Mark and I write our own material, earnest nineties alterna-pop numbers influenced by whatever it is we hear on the radio or in our classmates' cars or on mixtapes from girlfriends. None of it is jazz, though, so I don't talk about Athenaeum with Pete. He only knows that I play with some friends.

We record a few songs onto a reel-to-reel eight-track in the attic. Each part is performed impeccably, the recordings are made well, and the songs—if simple or naïve—are airtight little gems. And though I feel guilty admitting it, playing them with Mark is so much more satisfying than playing the old standards in For Pete's Sake. It is a truth that is impossible to deny because it is so viscerally apparent, like a chemical reaction within me.

One afternoon I decide to play our recordings for Pete. It's just gone on for too long and I want to share my excitement. We are in the attic. Pete is sitting in a chair at the worktable. I press play on the tape machine.

As soon as the music enters the room, Pete's eyes turn to the floor, and at once I know I've made a mistake. None of the things he is hearing, especially the aspects of the music at which Athenaeum excels—execution, control, tight pop craftsmanship—is something of value to Pete. What he looks for is much of the opposite—improvisation and innovation—and so now, in his company, Athenaeum's music has ceased to sound amazing to me and instead become an embarrassment. My discomfort grows with each passing note until finally I just stop the tape.

"You know, it's just rock and roll," I say, and Pete looks up, almost bashful. He knows what I'm feeling. He understands everything, all my guilt and embarrassment and my shame, as well as my pride and excitement, all without saying a word.

"It's . . . well recorded," he says, and we move on.

I'm the only person in For Pete's Sake who doesn't play a second instrument, but because we switch around during songs, I need something else I can play. Pete suggests hand drums. Bongos, congas, that type of thing. I only own bongos, though, so basically I just tap along on a pair of them every now and then while another drummer sits in on the kit, and while my bongo tapping is indeed enjoyable, it also gives me the opportunity to observe that I am not the best drummer in the band. Several of the other guys, some who don't even consider drums their main instrument, have surpassed me in skill. And it's not that their technique is better, although one of them—Will, a boy who I am good friends with, whose mother and sister are both professional musicians, and who lives in the most "bohemian" house of anyone I know, the house, in fact, where For Pete's Sake practices, in a basement so mildewy that my drums still smell like it for weeks after having been in there for a rehearsal—is indeed technically better at just about everything than I am. But the real difference between my drumming and everyone else's is that, ever since Athenaeum has come into my life, my *feel* for jazz—my swing—has started to falter. The nature of the rigid straight-eighths rock parts that I spend so many hours hammering away at with Mark has crept into the rest of my playing. I keep my concern in check, though, telling myself it's only a phase.

But the phase does not go away. As the months pass, my feel keeps getting worse and worse, until finally, in practice one afternoon when I'm back on the drum set, Pete stops the whole band.

He's looking at me.

"What?" I say.

Pete seems befuddled, almost unsure of how to explain.

"It's the accent," he finally says.

"What accent?"

"On the *two*. And the *four*," he says, like he is reminding me how it is that a human is supposed to breathe.

"What, what about it?" I say.

"It's wrong."

I try the ride pattern again—the pattern I've been playing for years. But Pete just shakes his head. I'm playing the correct notes, but somehow today they're not right.

Pete stands behind me, like he used to when I was a child. He wraps his arms around me, and with my hands in his, for the first time in years, he plays the part himself. Unlike those childhood lessons, though, when I felt invincible in his embrace, I'm fifteen years old now, and Pete is playing the part loudly and rapidly and in obvious irritation. I am so embarrassed that I cannot even tell the difference between Pete's ride pattern and mine, except for the fact that Pete's sounds annoyed, and when he lets go and I try the part again by myself, it sounds like nothing but rigid clanking.

"I'm sorry," I say.

Pete is never dismissive, never aggressive, never sharp. At all times he is reserved and in control. He returns to that place of quiet power now, letting the silence fill up the room.

"You just used to be this little jazz kid," he says quietly, in one final summary. He shakes his head gently, as if to say, it's OK, it's just over now. "You used to have this great feel, and now . . ."

The sentence does not end. It is clear where it is headed, though: to a place where my dream has become untangled with his.

A week or two later, Pete arrives at my house with a conga drum. It is his own, an original red-and-white fiberglass LP from the seventies. A glorious drum. I can still see him carrying it up my front walkway. When I open the door, he tells me that it can stay with me for a while, while I learn how to play it.

I'm shocked. I didn't ask for the drum. And surely Pete knows that my family could buy me one if I needed it. Still, he has taken this drum from his own house and brought it to me, unsolicited, almost like a peace offering.

I play the conga all afternoon, stopping only to back away

every now and then to admire it, squinting while turning my head to the side. It looks so cool I cannot bear it. At bedtime, I stand the drum beside my bed, just next to my head, and in the darkness reach out of the sheets to touch it. Finally, just before I sleep, I pull the drum closer and lay my palm on the head. I try to sleep with it that way, but each time I awake my hand has slipped off.

I find the comb in the seat of the couch one afternoon, after one of our talking lessons. It is wedged in the cushions where Pete was sitting. Its tines are a line of rigid metal spikes, and the handle is black plastic formed into a fist. I don't know at the time that this is an afro pick. I don't even know enough to think that it looks like a Black Power sign. All I know that it does not look like any comb I have ever seen before, and that it must be Pete's.

I wonder how I will return it to him. I feel like I can't say, "Hey Pete, I found this comb, is it yours?" because then it will be clear I am only pretending to be confused, because who else in my house would ever carry a comb like this? But if I say, "Pete, you left this comb on the couch," then I'll have to acknowledge the fact that we live in such disparate worlds that even something as normal as a comb from Pete's life is obviously his simply because it looks so unlike anything I ever even knew existed. It's like the whole divide between us is encapsulated in this one object, and it's a gulf I cannot bring myself to acknowledge, especially since it feels like we're growing further apart with each day. And so over the next couple weeks, I look at the comb from time to time, wondering what I should do with it.

If Pete is missing it. If maybe he even knows that he left it at my house and is too embarrassed himself to ask for it, for the same reasons I don't want to tell him I found it. Finally I just slip it into a drawer, but then in fear of my brother finding it there and asking me about it, I throw it away, hiding it at the bottom of the trash bag.

After we sell every copy of the Athenaeum cassette and then after we sell every copy of the self-released CD and then after we call the place listed in the back of *Tape Op* magazine to order another print run of one thousand discs, this is when the major label A&R reps—men with names like Craig and Hans and Gary—start flying in to see us perform. It all begins before I even graduate from high school, and by the time I'm eighteen, Athenaeum has become the most popular band in Greensboro. Maybe the most popular band the city has had in years. Ever? I'm not sure. Maybe.

There is no dramatic breaking off of things with Pete during this time, but at some point I no longer live in my mother's house, having moved into a dumpy rental with friends, and so where would our lessons take place? Sometimes I also wonder, if all these record labels want to give me a recording contract, do I really still need to be taking lessons? Occasionally, though, for a time, I will call to arrange a meeting with Pete, driving my drums back to my mother's house, where I set them up in the attic, trying to recreate the conditions of my youth, when those hours with Pete were the headiest and most important of my life. Our lessons are breezy and forgetful now, though. I take barely anything away from them.

In 1996, just before Athenaeum receives our first offer for a major label deal—the publishing contract with EMI—we play an outdoor festival in downtown Greensboro called City Stage. For Pete's Sake played the same event a year or two earlier, to a sparse crowd of parents and children. A large crowd has gathered for Athenaeum, though: several hundred young, affluent, and very healthy-looking white people, all of whom appear to have either just returned from college or are soon getting ready to go there.

Athenaeum will play hundreds of shows like this over the years. Very few remain in my memory. The details of this one are still sharp, though, because on this day I have learned that, for the first time since Mark and I formed the band, Pete will be coming to watch.

We are on a large stage erected in the middle of a downtown street. A group of fans—still a new development in Athenaeum's life—stand near the front, singing along. My friend Joey and his father are out there to the left, under a tree. My mother is nearby. A few of my housemates goof around with some girls. Nowhere can I find Pete, though, and for a moment I feel a swell of relief. Maybe he decided not to come after all. But then, a few songs into the set, I reach for my water and find Pete standing behind me. I do not know how long he has been there. What he has done, though, is much more than come to a show; he has positioned himself to see every movement I make. Viewed from the front, a drummer is like a pilot seen through a windshield, but from the back, everything is revealed. Pete has placed himself inside the cockpit.

At once, the dramatic cymbal crashes I have been smacking become embarrassing stage moves. Drum fills that consist of nothing but machine-gun sixteenth notes on the snare drum, which only minutes ago were thrilling in their rock and roll simplicity, now feel like the forced act of a clown. I cannot change my parts, though. Unlike in jazz, there is no room for improvisation in Athenaeum's music. Each note is a cog in our finely calibrated machine. And so I carry on, putting on the show that I must, knowing that as I do so, Pete is absorbing each stroke.

By the time we finish, I am burning with embarrassment. The backstage has filled up with people. Pete watches as they rush up to greet me. I laugh at their compliments and thank them. I give hugs. I shake hands. But each of these acts feels like torture under Pete's gaze, which, as always, is hidden behind his dark glasses.

Finally I make my way to him.

"It's just rock stuff," I say, an apology that can't come out fast enough.

"No no no," he says.

The whole world swells up between us. The memory of all that he taught me. About the importance of jazz. About how rock and roll holds such little reward for him. About race, and the South, and how all of it affected Pete's life. And yet despite all that here we are: standing backstage after my rock and roll concert, put on before a crowd of privileged white youth.

"You were sitting well," Pete finally says. "Your posture looked good."

My posture. Of all things, this is the one thing he can find to compliment me on. It's mortifying. Still, it's a rare bit of praise coming from Pete, and an elegant misdirection on his part, allowing us to both look away from what had become so abundantly clear: that I had not become the musician he once hoped that I would.

I've held on to Pete's compliment about my posture in the years that have passed. It was an embarrassment for me when he said it, but now it has transformed into something I carry around within myself, like a secret treasure, and take out from time to time to admire. Because even when I was little, Pete would talk about the importance of posture. How sitting the right way can free up your limbs.

"You should be able to lift a foot, even both, and your torso will not move," he would say, his hands on my shoulders, guiding me into position.

And even now, as I type, I'm lifting both feet from the floor, trying to keep my torso from moving. Seeing if I can still free my limbs. It's pointless, of course, since I'm not playing the drums—I barely do that anymore. I'm just sitting here at my computer. But maybe that's why I become so uncomfortable when the topic of my music career comes up nowadays. Because I've had a hard time moving on from all that Pete taught me. I'm holding on to it still, still thinking of him, still hoping to impress him, still holding my feet in the air, frozen.

3 | RADIANCE

It was that first night at Radiance, as I lay in my bed in the dark. I could hear my bandmates down the hall, laughing and playing some music. Bandmates? Maybe they were just roommates. The overlap was large and confusing. Chuck. Joey. Gill. Mark. Greg. Barrett. John Crooke. Grace. Hannibal. It's hard to even remember who all lived there over the years. The house was like a hostel for Greensboro musicians. Three bedrooms and one bath for $500 a month. Radiance is what we called it—that was the name of the street.

If I'd been at my mother's house, I would have been surrounded by silence. Here, though, on my first night out on my own, the commotion had been going on for so long, and my frustration building along with it, that I was reaching the point where I felt I might cry. I had to be at work at 7:00 a.m. I needed sleep. For one fleeting moment, I thought, screw it, I'm going back to my mom's house. I knew I couldn't do that, though. The nest had been flown. It was my first night away. To return now would be the ultimate humiliation. So I told myself I needed to grow up and just go ask my friends to be quiet. Bleary-eyed, wearing nothing but my underwear, I walked down the hall, only to find several young women on the couch with my friends.

"Nicky!" Barrett said, raising a can of Miller Lite in the air. Or maybe it was Joey who did this. Or Chuck. Or all of them. Doesn't matter. Whoever it was, the scene was tempting. Young women, friends, beer. The prospect of partying with these guys was already something I'd lived out so many times, though, that despite the temptation, my desire for sleep was still greater. So I didn't sit down. Instead I said, "Actually, you guys mind?"

And they said, "Oh, yeah, sure, no, sorry."

And then they toned it down.

And I went to sleep.

Anyone who knows me is like yeah, that's exactly what he did. I'm notoriously early to bed. But the point is there are moments in life when a hard turn is made. Moving out, getting a record deal, having a song appear on the radio. These are all events that will change a person, and they all happened to me, and they changed me. But what I'm struck with is all that did not change. That despite our youth and the things that were happening to us and getting ready to happen to us—not momentous in the scope of anything important to the world, but monstrously important to us as individuals—my bandmates and I all maintained a surprising consistency. We were serious about the sound of our instruments. There was much discussion of books and theater in that house. We were considerate. We looked out for one another. People would ask what the craziest thing was that we had done as a band, and we could not come up with an answer. This isn't to say we were nerds, although that term has become so ubiquitous and semi-"cool" that it's not even the right one to use anymore. We were just anchored to some calm core, and I think that core was each other. Almost everyone in the house I'd known since I was a child, so by the age of eighteen, on that first night at Radiance, I was already surrounded by very old friends. The world of Radiance was not one of rock and roll dreams. It was a world of innocence, but also one of wonder, and each room inside the house felt potent with magic.

The first bedroom I shared was with Gill, a tall, thin man who drove a yellow Plymouth Valiant and had the aura of a mystic. I remember waking early one morning to the sound of someone tossing a Ping-Pong ball against a wall, over and over again. I couldn't figure out where this was coming from. I even got up and looked out the window, trying to locate the source. Then Gill rolled over and I realized the sound wasn't a Ping-Pong ball at all—it was Gill breathing, making the smallest, strangest snore I've ever heard.

The next room I shared with Joey. In this one I slept on a bunk that was built for me by the carpenter for whom I was working at the time, a man named Matthew Butwinski. For some reason, though, Matthew had constructed the bed so close to the ceiling that once you were up there, you couldn't sit up. One afternoon, while I was lying up there and listening to Wilco's first album, I licked a stamp and stuck it to the ceiling. It was an old blue Canadian postage stamp with Queen Elizabeth on it that I'd found in the attic. Every night that stamp floated just above me, inches away, a dark rectangle against a vast field of gray.

Mark moved in after Joey left, taking the bed below. He was the singer of our band.

My new girlfriend visited me one night, and up there on my bed in the darkness—our foreheads touching, just inches away from that stamp—she whispered for the first time that she loved me.

The next morning, in the van on the way to a show, Mark said, "I love you, Nic. Nic, I love you." He'd heard the whole thing.

On another night I stood in the kitchen by the sink, talking with Gill as he sliced up an apple. Even before the knife slipped, I knew what would happen. I could see it in advance, like some premonition. The blade would move too quickly through the apple and slice into the space between his thumb and his forefinger, blood shooting onto his shirt. It happened just like I knew that it would, and then Gill wrapped his hand in a dirty dish towel and telephoned his father, a doctor, who arrived to drive him to the emergency room. After they left, the rest of us sat in the living room, shocked, watching a Mike Tyson boxing match, when to our surprise Gill stepped back through the door only a few minutes later, still covered in blood, still clutching the same dirty towel.

"My dad got in a wreck out front," he said and sat down. It was like we were invincible. We just watched the rest of the fight.

Everything happened at Radiance. We met record executives there, we celebrated our record deal in the kiddie pool, we fell in love.

Eventually I moved into the room at the back. It was the largest bedroom and I had it to myself. There was knotty faux pine paneling, a dingy wine-red carpet, and two large windows looking into a thicket of pines. I had no furniture beyond a mattress on the floor and my drum stool. The stereo sat on the carpet against the far wall. By this point we'd all been able to quit our day jobs because of the publishing advance, so time stretched out endlessly now. I would lie on the mattress looking out at the trees, watching the light fade from evening to dusk, listening to *Trampoline* by Joe Henry. *The Bends* by Radiohead. A Nil Lara record. That first Son Volt album.

Greg found a strange piece of furniture in the crawl space when he moved in. It was like a bookcase, but each shelf was only an inch or two tall. Perhaps it had once sorted mail.

"Would you like to see my shelves?" he would ask visitors. He became strangely attached to the thing.

One night, when Greg's younger sister came to visit, they got into an argument. I left to eat dinner with a friend and when I returned, I saw flames flickering out back, among the pines. I found Greg there, alone in the darkness, watching his shelves as they burned.

"My sister shook the gasoline out of the lawn mower onto them," he said. "And then . . ."

He spoke as if in a trance.

Finally, Barrett moved in. Barrett was gaunt, about six foot four, wore his hair in a type of pompadour, and had incredibly large lips. He drew apt comparisons to both Mick Jagger and Sandra Bernhard. (Later, after my tastes became more cosmopolitan, I realized who he really looked like was Jean-Paul Belmondo.) People loved him. "Athenaeum," they would say years later. "Wasn't that Barrett's band?" And yet he never even played an instrument. Barrett was only our road manager. The only musical input I ever received from him was during sound check, when he would tell me to go "play the clang boom chickaboom" or "hit that bang bang crash."

In his off time, Barrett invented the Doo-Key. This was a plastic piece of dog poop in which one could hide a house key. Barrett actually manufactured a fair number of these things, going so far as to hire a cartoonist to draw up a label. The packaging operation was set up in my bedroom, where in the evenings we would listen to music and drink beer while slipping Doo-Keys into their plastic sacks.

For a month or so, Barrett also made bombs. This was a fad that overwhelmed the whole house. Like a fever it ran through us all. We just couldn't stop. Barrett's bombs weren't actual bombs, though. They were just plastic soda bottles filled with some type of solution that would fizz dramatically once you dropped in a piece of tinfoil. If you screwed the lid on quickly enough, the whole thing would explode from the pressure. Endlessly, it seemed, we would throw Barrett's bombs into the night, where they popped like gunfire out in the dark. It must have sounded like a shootout to the rest of the block. Still, the neighbors didn't seem too concerned. They even came out and joined us sometimes. The older newspaper deliveryman who lived next door. The line cook, his roommate. It was like they all knew that we couldn't be dangerous, as if the whole world understood we were just making noise, that for this house all it took was a new sound going bang bang crash in the night to change the course of our lives.

4 | THE FAKE ID

According to its website, Oakwood corporate housing in the Hollywood Hills is the "number one choice for child actors and their parents," a metric that seems impossible to determine. Is there a census of child actors? I, for one, never saw any while I was there. And though I was not a child during the months that I lived at Oakwood—over the late winter and into the early spring of 1997—nor was I an actor, I was close enough to being a child that I could not legally purchase alcohol or enter many of the establishments that served it.

I was, in other words, nineteen.

"This is ridiculous," our label rep said one afternoon when, after suggesting the band meet a producer that evening at a bar, someone pointed out I wouldn't be allowed past the door. Incredulous—almost offended, even, at the suggestion that any law could apply to us—she looked around the room and said, "Can't someone just get him a fake ID?"

Two days later I found myself buckled into the passenger

seat of a rental Ford Explorer with Barrett, our road manager, as he backed into an illegal parking spot in front of a strip mall.

"Nicky," he said. "It's time to wang chung."

What this meant, in Barrett-speak, was that business of the illegal variety was about to take place. And though Barrett was the most unusual and dangerous person I knew, he also seemed to exude such a consistent level of confidence that I never felt anything but safe with him, so dutifully I followed him up a flight of stairs to a door that advertised "novelties."

Inside, a young man stood at a counter.

"Yeah, my boy Nicky here," Barrett said, laying a hand on my shoulder, "he's gonna be needing a novelty driver's license."

I don't recall how the intel on this place came to Barrett—maybe the label provided it, maybe someone at the studio, or more likely he just picked it up through his inherent radar for illicit activity—but regardless, our desires were clear. The man took my photo in front of a blue curtain and then asked me my name and birthdate, to which I replied with my actual name and birthdate, only adjusting the year back by two when I remembered the whole point of this criminal exercise. As for my address, though, I just said "whatever."

Two minutes later, I was an unsmiling twenty-one-year-old with a Class C Texas driver's license #31209121 who lived at 1281 S Main Street in Dallas, TX 77212.

I was shocked. This ID didn't look fake at all. It even had a shimmery hologram of the Lone Star state seal printed into its matte plastic laminate. Something about the convincing nature of the object made the whole enterprise feel suddenly much more illegal. It was like I expected a spy to emerge at any second and hand me my next assignment. Main Street, though—that was the one false note, and for a second I even considered asking the man for another card, one without such an obviously fake-sounding address. He was already cleaning up, though, and I was the one who'd told him to come up with it on his own in the first place, so we paid up and left.

Outside, a pink parking ticket was waiting for us under the wiper. Barrett wasn't concerned. He just pulled it out and crumpled it up, the same thing he'd been doing for weeks. The car had been rented by someone at Atlantic Records, after all. We didn't know whose name was attached to it, just that it wasn't one of ours. So Barrett tossed the ticket into the trash and away we drove, two criminals at large in the city.

Fake IDs. Their name alone conjures a potent underworld of teenage contraband. Lumpy dog-eared driver's licenses passed down from one teenager to another, some with the dates adjusted in ballpoint pen or with the laminate peeled off and a Rite Aid passport photo slipped in between. I remember once when a friend even forged a note from his mother saying "Greg is 21" and gave it to the kind Indian man behind the register at my neighborhood Hop-In, along with a six-pack. The ploy didn't work (the attendant called out "he has a note!" after which the manager appeared and considered the document for a surprisingly long time before finally shaking his head), but the point is that it didn't seem entirely impossible that it *wouldn't* work. It felt like, in those days—in the mid-nineties—all you needed was *something*, maybe even just a piece of paper saying you were twenty-one, and the elusive pleasures of adulthood could be yours.

The idea of getting a fake ID for myself, though, was never something I had really considered. Using them was utterly illegal, for one thing, and I was a risk-averse young man. Which is not to say I did not drink illegally inside bars. I did so almost every night. It's just that I drank inside bars where I was performing, which meant the bars themselves were the ones providing me with the drinks, and free ones at that. So why would I bother?

That was the logic of my old world, though. The one in Greensboro, North Carolina. The one where I was a teenage drummer in a moderately successful local band, hoping for a break. The one where, only a year and a half before, I'd been such a law-abiding do-gooder that I'd been elected student body president of my high school and gotten in to Princeton and Columbia. But I said no to those schools. In fact, I said no to attending any school *at all*, a decision seemingly insane from the perspective of my world today, but which at the time made perfect sense to me, because before I was even out of high school it was starting to feel like an inevitability that my band would sign a major label record deal, and that is indeed what we'd done. So I was no longer student body president. I was no longer even a student. I was a nineteen-year-old drummer now, one with a recording contract with Atlantic Records and an apartment at Oakwood corporate housing in the Hollywood Hills. It was like I was a totally different person from who I had been before, and now I had the ID to prove it.

Still, I never went to a bar. Not in LA. All I did was go to the studio, every day, morning to night. Everything I cared about was inside its walls.

Master Control was the name of the place, and it was

comically ugly. Part of a semi-industrial strip mall in Burbank, it felt more like the loading dock of a dollar store than a recording studio. At first, I was disappointed by its homely façade, but I got over that quickly, because inside Master Control the walls were hung with gold records, dark corners glittered with instruments, and other musicians came in and out, some even to play on our record, including an accordion player named James who arrived in a vintage green Mercedes one day, wearing a suit, accompanied by his beautiful wife. He was a member of the Irish band the Pogues. I'd never seen a person look so cool in my life.

What I see now, though, when I think back on that studio, is not the dapper accordion player or those gold records that hung on the walls. What I see is the morning sun shining into the lobby, striped thin through the blinds. Take-out breakfast is waiting, steam from the coffee catching pale in the light. I eat in silence, flipping through one of the industry magazines on the table. I don't even know what it says. All I'm thinking about are the drum parts I'll be performing that day.

"Nic?" Gavin says, sticking his head through the door.

Gavin is our producer, a dour Scottish man with braces on his teeth that he covers with the tip of his tongue when he laughs.

"OK," I say, and fold the magazine shut.

I follow him into the dark hallway, like I'm being called into an appointment by a nurse, as if I'm a man with a longstanding condition who has been waiting his entire life just to show someone what it is that I've caught.

After the album was finished, we returned to North Carolina, where I left my hometown and moved fifty miles east to Chapel

Hill. Home to the state's flagship university, Chapel Hill was also the center of the world's musical universe, at least as far as I was concerned. Its thriving congregation of arty weirdos was so contrary to the state's otherwise conservative milieu that the legendary super-racist North Carolina senator Jesse Helms once suggested that rather than fund the state zoo they just erect a fence around Chapel Hill instead. Ben Folds Five and the Squirrel Nut Zippers were both based out of there, and both had scored recent radio hits, and there was a seemingly endless list of other local bands too—like Dillon Fence, Southern Culture on the Skids, Archers of Loaf, and Superchunk—who were all making such a name for themselves nationally that people had started to call the place "the next Seattle." Greensboro, on the other hand—where I'd been living since I was three—had felt so dead to me for so long that I'd called it "Greensboring" for years.

Problem was, Chapel Hill's music scene was utterly inaccessible to me, closed off behind bar doors and bouncers. The 506, Henry's, the Cave, the Orange County Social Club, the Cat's Cradle . . . All these places required an ID to enter them, and so I finally started to use mine.

Some people still swoon at the names of baseball players they followed in their youth, or the ex-girlfriends of older brothers, but to me, the musicians I met in Chapel Hill during this time are the ones that will forever fill me with awe. John Plymale. Greg Humphreys. Chris Phillips. Darren Jessee. Dave Burris. Jimbo Mathus. Mac McCaughan. John Howie Jr. John Gillespie. Scott Carle. The list goes on. I'd have a drink with one of them one night, then tune in to the *Tonight Show* a couple days later and see them perform. The guy who drove me to the garage to pick up my broken Karmann Ghia would be in the pages of the *Rolling Stone* in my mailbox when I got home. It was incredible to have such access to so many musicians I idolized, and it was with great seriousness that I studied how each of them spoke, what they wore, and what music they were listening to. There was a sophistication to them all that was thrilling and new to me. One songwriter I got to know was the first man I'd ever met who called himself a feminist. Another kept clippings from *Harper's* tacked up on his fridge. There were drummers who seemed more interested in obscure films than their own bands, and I knew several guitarists around town who effortlessly mixed international politics and basketball into the same conversation. So while my former high school classmates were busy discovering their own new identities down the street in the dorm rooms and lecture halls of UNC, I was doing the same thing at the 506, or backstage at the Cat's Cradle, or at a small table on the side porch of Henry's. These were my classrooms, and that fake ID was my ticket into them.

I changed. Of course I did. I was trying to. I was primed to. I was the right age to change. But what I didn't expect from all the transformations I underwent during this period was that one of them would include how I felt about my own band. For the first time, though, I started to imagine what it might be like to play in a different band, one perhaps more like those I now spent my nights listening to and hanging out with in Chapel Hill. These were bands that didn't seem interested in writing songs for the radio, even though many of them did enjoy radio hits. Instead they seemed much more intent on making music that was unusual, or smart, or shocking. And these were all things my band was not. We were unimpeachably sincere.

We invested deeply in the quality of our musical performances. We cared above all about the craft of our songs. And while these are worthwhile and meaningful assets, they had ceased to be the things I was most excited about. It was an awareness I resisted acknowledging at first, but like a dark invasion of rot, it wouldn't stop spreading.

I awoke often during this time to the ringing of the telephone. These calls would come in at hours during which it was frankly embarrassing to still be asleep. Eleven in the morning. Noon. Sometimes later. If I answered—and I always tried to answer, worried that the call might be some type of important band business, which sometimes it was—my voice was invariably frogged up with sleep. So I developed a technique. I'd say "hello" over and over again before I picked up. "Hello, hello, hello," I'd say, starting before I'd opened my eyes. "Hello, hello, hello," I'd say, into the dim daylight coming through the closed blinds. "Hello, hello, hello, hello," I'd say, with each word shedding a little bit more of the sleep from my voice, until finally I sounded like the Nic Brown I was before I came to this place, the one who slept normal hours and lived in Greensboring and wasn't yet twenty-one. The one who still loved his band without reservation. Only then would I pick up the phone, as if I'd just been waiting for that person to call, and say, "Hello?"

I turned twenty-one in Birmingham.

I turned twenty-one in Houston.

I turned twenty-one in San Antonio.

We were flying between shows at this point, and those were the cities we hit on that day—April 25, 1998. At midnight on

April 24, though—the very moment my fake ID expired—I was onstage in Birmingham. My band had already performed, but the singer of the headlining act, a band from New Orleans named Cowboy Mouth—the rare group with a lead-singing drummer—had called me up to play his drums so he could roam the crowd while he sang. This man was named Fred and he dressed in torn overall jean shorts, scream-sang like an insane hillbilly caveman, and was known for spraying audience members in a constant and confusing mist of saliva and sweat. On this night, though, at the moment the clock struck twelve, Fred paused his wild act long enough to demand that the whole crowd—several thousand people—sing "Happy Birthday to Nic."

Or at least that's what it sounded like. I knew that there was an extra K on that Nick, though, because in a strange twist of fate, the crowd wasn't singing for me. Fred just happened to have another friend at the show that night named Nick—a woman, actually—who shared the same birthday. Afterward, though, when my band members all thought the song was for me, I didn't correct them. "Yeah," I said. "Pretty cool, huh?" It was my name, after all, and it was my birthday, and I was onstage before everyone who was singing it, so why not claim the song as my own? Still, the charade left me feeling empty, as if another fake ID had made a surprise appearance at the very moment my old one expired.

Every morning during this time, a man named Gary would wake me in a discount hotel. I would follow him out to the van, put on my headphones, and fall back asleep.

We navigated with road atlases and pencils. We did not have

cell phones. Maybe Gary did, but it was for business. The rest of us used payphones when we needed to, but usually we didn't need to. We just floated around the country in our own silent cloud. We filmed an interview for CNN and never saw it. People told us we were on MTV; we didn't see it. I did phoners with local dailies over the hotel room lines, but never knew if they made it into print. At a gas station in Virginia I bought a *Rolling Stone* that included a photo of me, and in a burst of excitement and loneliness I had the sudden urge to tell the young woman behind the counter that I was in it, but when I reached the register I became overwhelmed with embarrassment and purchased the magazine in silence.

Each new town looked the same: a parking lot and a club. There was no time to see more. At night, the lights imparted some type of magic to these rooms, but afternoons revealed what they really were: dilapidated bars that smelled like spilled beer. The stretch between sound check and showtime, though—those were the hours I stole for myself.

One day after sound check I went for a walk with a Dwight Yoakam CD on my headphones. The music I listened to that year was by nature oblique like this, unrepresented in the collections of people I knew. I escaped into the odd cultural corners of free albums provided by various label reps. It was like the lessons of Chapel Hill had complicated any chance I had to enjoy the music of bands in our orbit, so instead I found myself listening to anything that seemed outside my judgment; hence the Dwight Yoakam.

I ended up in a cracked and empty parking lot behind some shuttered industrial building. I think this was in Cincinnati. I was a few blocks away from the venue. We had seven hours till showtime. The lot was empty and felt like it had been for decades. I just sat there on the loading dock in the dappled sunlight of a tree whose limbs had been broken by truck traffic, swinging my legs and listening to Dwight Yoakam. That world! Where was the danger? I didn't see it. I can't believe how innocent it all was. It was like the country was just a series of empty concrete surfaces, all stretched out before me, just waiting for me to step onto them and look around. I hoped against hope that that night's show would be canceled, dreaming of some way I could stay on that loading dock, listening to Dwight Yoakam, forever.

Later that summer we played at an amphitheater, opening for a popular band with whom we were touring. They had the number one song in the country. The members were all very nice and two of the three wore eyeliner. They were somewhat famous for their hair. Before the show, backstage, my band had argued about who we were going to allow to travel with us on our new tour bus. Girlfriends, friends, family? We agreed the best policy was to take no one. Our singer, however, one of the most considerate people I knew, wanted to bring his girlfriend. She was kind and made all of us happy. We'd only have that bus for one month. But we didn't know that yet. We thought it was our permanent world and we were intent on securing its borders. Our capacity to give what we should to one another had run low. So we told him it wasn't a good idea to bring anyone on the bus, not even his girlfriend.

Onstage that night, because of the lights, I saw nothing beyond the first rows of spectators. There were thousands of people there, yet I was unclear on the count by tens of thousands. It was ten thousand, or twenty. Or more? Somebody said it was more. Amphitheaters are like playing in a sea of novocaine. Despite the volume all sound is diffuse. Everything is too far away. So as the population of a small city cheered, I barely noticed. What I did was think about how unfair it was of us to have told our singer not to bring his girlfriend, but I couldn't imagine a way to admit that to him now. Or maybe this wasn't the night we talked about that. Maybe this was another night, the night we argued about tempos. It doesn't matter. What matters is that I didn't even know I was playing. It was like I was just sitting alone up there, thinking about some regrets.

At the close of the set, we played our hit song. It opened with four measures of thump—the snare drum cracking on each quarter note: bang bang bang bang. I launched into it and the crowd began to bounce, jumping in rhythm to each beat. I still remember the light. The sky glowed a faint ochre, backlighting in silhouette a sea of bouncing heads. I am ashamed to admit what I thought at the time. How do I say this? I had run out of compassion for the music, for myself, for the audience even. I looked out at the crowd and, in my least charitable moment, asked, *Why are any of you here?* It felt like anyone who wanted to jump along to the music I was playing was someone with whom I could never spend time.

I went on to play music for years. I worked other very good jobs for other major labels, played with excellent bands, performed on the *Tonight Show*, recorded for films, and made a decent living. I'm a good drummer. But I guess that night was when I knew my career with Athenaeum was over.

Near the end of the summer, I bumped into a young man in a parking lot behind a theater. I knew the guy somehow. He was a friend of a friend, and it felt good to make even that tenuous connection while out on the road. The man was seemingly lost, though, and explained to me that he'd just been turned away from the door because he wasn't yet twenty-one.

I thought about my fake ID, which was still in my wallet, and how it had gotten me out of so many similar predicaments. Then a sudden surge of benevolence swelled up within me.

"Here," I said, pulling the card out of my pocket. "Use this."

"What?" the guy said.

"Yeah, keep it. I don't need it anymore."

A big dumb grin spread across the man's face as he realized what it was that he held. I told him the story behind the ID, how I'd gotten it in LA after the label had asked me to, and the tale seemed to make the whole thing even better for him. It felt right and good what I was doing, and I told myself I had bestowed a special gift upon this young man, one he would treasure forever.

As soon as the guy jogged away, though, all of my self-satisfaction disappeared. What would happen if he got caught with it, I thought. My actual name and photo were on that ID. I started to pace the lot, searching for him, while visions of the fiasco played out in my mind. The news would pick it up. "Drummer Arrested for Distributing Fake ID," they'd say. The label would get involved. My parents. I started walking more quickly now, becoming increasingly frantic, forcing myself not to run. There were people all around, and I didn't want to look like a panicked crazy person in front of them. But I felt like a panicked crazy person. Still, I couldn't find the man anywhere, and eventually, after several minutes of frantic hunting, I just gave up and stood panting at the back of the lot. There was a dumpster half-covered in vines there, with a dark grove of trees stretching beyond it, their trunks sprinkled with trash. Potato chip bags. Old beer cans. Cigarette butts. I stared into that mess as the late afternoon sun set, my heart still pounding in fear. That fake ID was long gone. All I was left with now was my real identity, the thing I'd had all along, but what did that even mean? I had changed so much in so little time that I barely even knew who I was. I didn't want to go back to who I had been, though. That's not what this was about. The reason my heart was racing so hard was because of all that might happen next.

5 | THE YIPS

It's 3:00 a.m. and I'm back on the edge of a bathtub, naked and sweaty and tired. This is in a Motel 6 after the show. Or it's in a Budget Inn. Or maybe an Econo Lodge. Or all them, actually. This happens in them all.

I open the faucets—all the way, both knobs—and the air starts to fill up with steam. I can still see the bathwater, though. I can feel the force of it pummeling the plastic tub beneath me. And I know what sound it is making—a hard roaring hiss. But that isn't the sound that I hear. What I hear is a low muffled hum, like a pillow has been pressed firmly against both of my ears.

I wonder if this is what a drug addict feels like, looking at a tooth that's just fallen out, or some other evidence of self-destruction. Blood on the sink. Track marks. I don't know. At least I'm not a drug addict. For me, though, this difference between what I know I should be hearing and what I am actually hearing is my own nightly proof of self-destruction, because it's a reminder of how hard I am hitting the drums. And though I am aware that I am playing my instrument too loudly—and that it is destroying not only my ears, but the very songs I am performing on—I cannot find a way to stop.

I pinpoint one afternoon as the catalyst for all this. It happens a few months earlier, before the bathwater loses its hiss. We're at sound check in San Antonio, at the Sunken Garden Theater, playing the first of a few shows with Foo Fighters, and while I'm indifferent to the band—they're fine—I am curious about their drummer. The front man is Dave Grohl, after all, who played drums in Nirvana, so I want to see who Nirvana's drummer has hired to be his own drummer. The guy's name is Taylor Hawkins, and up on the riser before me, he looks like a surfing supermodel—all blond hair and jawbone and sinew.

"Snare drum," the soundman says.

And then Taylor Hawkins hits his snare drum, and that's all that it takes. One note. He's just hit the drum so hard, and with such elegance and explosive grace, that at once I think, *That's what I'll do. I'll just start hitting harder.* Because at this moment in my life, I'm desperate for any new inspiration, and within that void Taylor Hawkins's one loud note on the snare drum has just appeared and it sounds utterly thrilling.

What has happened to me is that the bands I've loved in the past—including my own—have begun to lose their allure. It's like I've just started thinking about being unfaithful to them, unable to resist an attraction to others. My friends at Atlantic, our record label, have picked up on this development at least a little bit, because already they know I don't want them to send me free rock CDs anymore. I want the weird stuff now, the arty stuff, the difficult and strange stuff. Philip Glass's score to *Dracula*. Olu Dara's old man songs. Cesária Évora singing about Cape Verde in some language I don't know. The Kronos Quartet. Caetano Veloso. I even take the CD discards from radio stations we visit, stuff that's too weird to air, like a double album of artists reading Edgar Allan Poe stories or an album from a band named Skeleton Key whose drummer plays pieces of trash.

My own band is nothing like these acts. We're a pop band. A good one, but my passion for the project has faded. It's like that period of a love affair when you know the relationship is dying, yet still you search for some way to revive it. And this is when I see Taylor Hawkins. This is when I decide to hit hard.

It's a summer afternoon. Bright sunlight bears down on a crowd of thousands. This is a few months later and we're onstage at an amphitheater in Indianapolis, in the middle of the first chorus of the first song.

By this point, I've been hitting the drums so hard that I'll find a spray of blood across the snare drum some nights. My fingers have blistered. And the bathwater has just begun to sound muffled at night. Still, a minor thrill has returned to my performances because of it, and other drummers have started to offer compliments. I even read an article recently in which the drummer of another band said his favorite drummers are "Taylor Hawkins from the Foo Fighters, and Nic from Athenaeum." So as my enthusiasm for our band's music continues to decrease, I keep hitting harder.

I'm not thinking about any of that right now, though. What

I'm thinking about are my drumsticks, which are slipping out of my hands, and my bass drum, which is sliding away from me because I'm playing it like I'm trying to kill it.

Mark, our singer, looks over his shoulder and mouths the words "slow down."

I tell myself to forget the drumsticks, to ignore the bass drum. That I need to focus on the song that I'm playing. That I have to listen to the needs of the band. I decrease our tempo, hoping to bring it down to the right speed, but after playing only another verse or so, Mark turns around and says now it's too slow.

It is the same thing that happened the day before. And the day before that. And the day before that. But no matter what, I can't find the right tempo.

From time to time I hear about baseball pitchers who get "the yips," a condition where they can no longer control their pitches. They try to throw a strike down the middle and instead hit the backstop. Their curveball won't curve. A sinker will rise. It's a classic performance disfunction based on overthinking, and I believe what is happening to me during this time is something like that. I think I've gotten the yips.

It's clear to me even while it is happening that my heavy hitting is part of the problem. It has ruined my technique, which has thrown off my feel, and in turn completely messed with my sense of tempo. It would be as if one dancer in a troupe suddenly started to move with the most extreme motions possible, all while not listening to the music. Of course he would be out of sync with the others. But even though I understand this, I still cannot bring myself to stop hitting the drums so hard, because if I give that up, then what will be left for me? It feels like the only part of the music that can still bring me joy.

During the rest of the show, Mark keeps turning around, telling me my tempos are off, just like he has for weeks, and I keep trying to fix them and fail, just like I have for weeks, until finally, at the end of the set, my confidence is so shot that I just count us in to a song at the wrong tempo on purpose, hoping somehow it will be right.

I open my eyes, still filled with dread. In the dream, Mark kept looking over his shoulder, again and again, telling me the tempos were off. It is a spring morning. March. The windows are open. I can hear children across the street at Guy B. Phillips Middle School screaming as they get picked up by their parents. Then I realize it isn't morning. It's the middle of the afternoon.

I'm home from the tour now, but for weeks tempos have still been the first thing on my mind. I lay in my bed like this each day, staring at the ceiling, dreading the next show. This morning, though, something has broken. I get out of bed, determined to find some way to release myself from the cycle.

I pull a file from my desk. In it are two of my old college acceptance letters. One from Princeton and one from Columbia, such thrilling messages to have received when they first came. I feel a sadness as I hold them in my hands now, though. It was five years ago that they were mailed to me, and at the time I said no. I did take a one-year deferral from Columbia, even convincing them to let me stretch it out for a second year, but I never called back after that. Now I feel like a fool.

The Princeton letter has one word at the top, printed in

bold: YES! I wonder if the phone number on the letterhead is still even in service, and if it is, what someone who isn't in high school might say to the person who answers. I read recently about the singer for the band Weezer going to Harvard, though, and it has given me the idea that college might still be a possibility for me. So I pick up the phone and dial.

"Hello," I say, trying to sound both like an adult who is above all this, while at the same time a student who is very interested in attending. I'm not sure what either is supposed to sound like. "I got in there a few years back but have actually been working as a musician . . ." I pause here in hopes the woman on the other end might ask for more detail. She remains silent. "And it looks like I'll have some time this fall, so I was thinking about reapplying."

"Got in when?" she says.

"Ninety-five."

"Wow. OK. Yeah, well, if you got in once, I guess that's a good sign, but . . . Can you hold for a second?"

"Sure," I say, because what else do I have to do? I watch the middle schoolers climb into their parents' cars.

"OK," she says, coming back. She sounds like she has information now. Her voice is confident and assured. "So, what you'll need to do first is take the SATs again. Those scores expire after four years . . ."

And then she keeps talking, but I stop listening after "SAT." Take the SAT again? I'm not taking the SAT again. That would be a disaster. The phone call comes to an end in a blur, and by the time I hang up, I'm already mourning the dream.

The Columbia letter is still in front of me, though. And they have a phone number too. Why not, I think, and I dial.

"Yeah, you have to reapply," the Columbia officer says. She's all business.

"OK, thanks, yeah," I say. I came to this conversation pre-defeated.

But then she says, "If you deferred, though, I don't know, maybe you still have a file? What's your name again?"

"Nic Brown. Nicholas Brown."

"Let me see if I can pull it."

As I wait, I stare at the last students getting picked up out on the street. The kids who I attended middle school with have all already graduated from college by now, I think. Not many musicians I know ever went, though. At least not all the way through. Maybe one or two.

"Nicholas?" the officer says, picking back up. "I actually have your file right here, and I have good news. Looks like you're still enrolled."

"What?"

She laughs. "Yeah."

"What does that mean?"

"It means you can come in the fall."

I experience one of those rare moments that sends me forward in time, even while it is happening. I see myself in the future, thinking about how I'll remember this woman's words as she speaks them. How I will tell people it is the best news I've ever received.

"So," I say, "I can just come in the fall?"

"Yeah."

It's unclear to me if I have to tell this woman my intentions or not at this very moment, but I'm afraid of losing my chance, so I say, "I'd like to do that."

The band's calendar is booked with a long stretch of waiting. The new record won't be out for months. I tell Mark and Alex I'm going to school in the meantime. That I can travel to shows, come home for rehearsal if I need to. It's New York. Easy for me to get in and out of. They're fine with it. We aren't playing much at all during this stretch, so it really doesn't matter where I am. After one semester, I'll just take a leave again and go back on tour.

I start riding the Amtrak back and forth, from Durham to Penn Station, well before the semester. It's an eleven-hour ride, but I have nothing else on my schedule. I'm making the move mentally, dreaming the city's streets even while I am on them. At home, it feels like every aspect of my life has been taking up so much room. My drumsticks, my tempos, my fear of the next show. My brain is overcrowded with it all. In the city, though, vast spaces seem to open up around me, limitless room in which I can look away from all of that.

One day, while staying with my old road manager, Barrett, in his apartment on West 52nd Street, I run into an acquaintance from Greensboro, a guitarist named Alec who lives in the city now. I ask him who he's been playing with.

"Band called Skeleton Key," he says.

I almost gasp. It's one of the groups I've been listening to, a band so strange that, when I played their album for my friends in Chapel Hill who were into weird music, they all seemed to think it was too weird even for them. They hated it.

"I love that band," I say.

"Really?" Alec says. He seems surprised I know who they are. The band is on Capitol but about as unknown as a major label act can be. Still, they were nominated for a Grammy once, though it wasn't for music—it was for best album artwork, a footnote that seems a perfect encapsulation of their appeal, because to me the whole thing feels more like an art project than a band.

Alec gets a funny look on his face as he takes in my excitement. He raises an eyebrow.

"Actually, we do need a drummer," he says.

I don't go to the first Skeleton Key rehearsal telling them anything more than I'm going to be in New York for a few months and could possibly play a few shows if they needed. Still, I'm a fan of their music, something I can't say about most of the bands I've been sharing stages with. I'm excited at the prospect of even being in the same room with them.

Before we rehearse, though, I struggle to learn all the parts. This is before YouTube or anything, so I can't see how they were performed. I only have the CD to puzzle it out, and truly, I know next to nothing about the band. All I have is their music, and the drum parts are mystifying. Some sound like they're played on a drum set, some on pieces of trash, and most an unusual combination of the two. A lot of it sounds like scrap metal. I work out ways to fake the trash parts on my drum rims, the bells of cymbals, and even the sides of the drums themselves, putting in what I know is way too much time figuring out all the strange sticking patterns that they require. The parts are highly unusual. Most of all, though, I'm terrified my tempos will be off.

I meet the band at a rehearsal space in Dumbo, just south of the Brooklyn Bridge, which you can see from the windows.

The drums are classic rehearsal space junk. Funky heads, weird angles, half-broken hardware. Because of my yips, though, I'm already so uncomfortable behind my own drums that the idea of having to play other ones, especially crappy ones that sound different, look different, and feel different, seems almost impossible.

The singer, a tall man named Erik who has the smiling face of a kind Scandinavian farmer, is wearing vintage leather overalls made for Swedish motorcycle policemen. Or maybe it's Norwegian motorcycle policemen. Danish? I can't remember. Somewhere distant and cold. He owns the look. He seems utterly calm and cool and unlike anyone I have ever met before, and when I learn he's been playing with Yoko Ono and John Cale, it makes perfect sense.

We start the first song, but after only a few bars I find both Alec and Erik looking at me so strangely that I stop.

"What?" I say.

"You're doing both parts?" Erik says.

"Parts of what?"

"The trash and the drums?"

"I guess."

"Cause the trash guy played the part with the bell."

"OK."

"But the drums are just hat and the bass."

And then it becomes clear: *This* is why the parts had been so hard for me to learn—the band had two drummers. One on the set, the other on trash. I had no idea. I'd learned the parts of two drummers at once.

"Oh," I say, mortified. "OK. Yeah. I'll just play the drum set part then."

So we try it again, with me playing half of the part I prepared, but it doesn't feel very good.

"Actually, just do what you were doing before," Erik says.

So I go back to my first part, and Erik and Alec almost start laughing at all the insane patterns I've worked out. It's a bit of a drumming freak show. It sounds pretty good, though, and as the hour passes, I find that I'm not thinking about the strange kit I'm playing at all. I'm just playing. And while I'm hitting the drums hard, I'm not forcing anything like I had been with Athenaeum. It's not until well after we're done that I consider my tempos. They had been fine.

I tell Alex, our bass player, when I come home for Thanksgiving. I call him first, asking if we can talk. By the time I get to his house, I can tell he already knows what I'm going to say.

"I think I'm going to keep going to college," I say.

I've rehearsed it all in the car. I never use the word quit. Maybe my drum tech, Jeremy, can fill in, I say. It'll be fine, we agree. Alex is totally understanding. We even laugh about things. This is why I told him first, though, because I knew he would make it easy for me. I've used him as a trial run. Mark is the one I am worried about. Not that I'm concerned Mark will get angry—he's one of the most even-tempered people I know—but he's the one who I started the band with. He's the one I dreamed each step of this journey with, from playing my eighth-grade dance to signing a record deal to then, incredibly, scoring a hit. To tell him I'm quitting now will be the real end of things, and I guess that's what I'm afraid of.

I drive to Mark's house. I'm sure I do that. And I know that

I tell him I'm quitting. But it's funny what memory retains. It's a fickle editor, leaving some unexpected scenes on the cutting room floor, sometimes even the ones we'd thought would be most important. So while I have an image of sunlight on Alex's car window from that day, and a vision of his mother in the living room waving to me as I arrive, I can remember nothing about telling Mark.

I know I haven't repressed the memory because it was traumatic. I would have remembered if there'd been a scene. I think I just don't remember it now because the moment itself didn't matter. It was only the inevitable conclusion to something that we both knew was coming, something that had become so obvious over such a long period of time that quitting was just the final acknowledgement. Mark knows me so well, in fact, that he probably could have told me I was quitting long before I knew it myself.

Later that week, an article runs in the *Greensboro News & Record*. "Athenaeum's Drummer Leaves Band for School" reads the headline.

"How can I be angry?" Mark tells the reporter. "[Nic] has been very dedicated for a decade. He put off going to school, and it's not like a community college. Now, it's time for him to move on, and we'll pull together and move forward."

Diplomatic and supportive. That's all Mark ever is. But if his feelings were hurt, and they might well have been, I don't think it happened on the day that I quit. I think it would have happened well before that, during that long stretch of time when our tempos were heading off in two different directions, almost as if the music itself was telling us where we would go.

6 | POOF

A colleague introduces me to a woman visiting campus. We're in the lobby on the first floor of my office building, right beside the dean's office. I've just come out of the stairwell and I can see the secretary on the other side of the glass. I feel a bit on display, exposed.

"This is Nic!" my coworker says. "He's our resident rock star."

We laugh. Or the woman and my friend laugh. I look down.

"I'm serious," my colleague says. "He used to be a drummer."

"Oh yeah?" the woman says. "Who'd you play for?"

The woman is older. A wide cashmere scarf is draped over her shoulders, the shade of an almond. There's a sophistication here. She's visiting from Yale, so she carries with her the glamour of a more prestigious institution. She is a celebrated writer. I read a piece of hers in *The Paris Review* recently, in which she mused about the hidden passageways of blood pulsing within us. I thought it was excellent.

"Oh, I played with a lot of different people," I say. I let my eyes drop again. "That was my former life."

She reads my discomfort and lets the topic drop. I wonder if her ability to tell I'm uncomfortable so quickly is part of what makes her such a fine writer, if it's an indication of some heightened sensitivity on her part. Whatever it is, I'm grateful for it, and when I have dinner with her later that evening the topic doesn't come up.

If I'd answered her, though, I would have mentioned Athenaeum, Skeleton Key, Longwave, Eszter Balint, Ben Lee, Matt Pond PA. Those are a few of the acts. Maybe you know one or two. Probably not. That's why I never tell anyone. It embarrasses me to have to explain that they were once important, at least to me, and though I guess none of them really changed the world, back then—in the late 1990s and early 2000s, especially when I was living in New York City and working as a sideman—they were the pinnacle of my career. It was during this time, though—around 2003, when I was twenty-five—that three things happened, each of which by itself was just an event, but together started to change the way I thought about my job.

1.

The first was just after a guy I knew died. It was one of those things where he had been sitting in a car for too long in the same position and when he stood up a blood clot that had formed in his legs shook loose and floated up and into his heart. Pulmonary embolism is what it's called. Terrible, like being struck by an invisible bolt of lightning. His name was Justin and he was tall and handsome and athletic and only twenty-eight years old. Basically the picture of invincibility. He made it all the way into our friend Charles's apartment on 52nd Street before he collapsed.

To me Justin was just an acquaintance, but he was one of Charles's close friends, so when Justin's mother asked Charles to help clean out Justin's storage space, I went along for support. We were told to take what we wanted. I didn't want any of this stuff, though. It was all just plastic laundry baskets, halogen lamps, nylon gym bags. That type of thing. But then I saw the sleeping bag. And I needed a sleeping bag.

As a sideman, you must know your parts, of course, but you also have to be able to travel light, travel easy, and sleep on a floor when you need to. The fact that I didn't own a sleeping bag meant that I was always asking people for help, though, and it made me feel conspicuous, and unprofessional, and those were the last things I wanted to be, because the best sidemen just disappear. They recede into the song when they play, and when they travel, you don't even know that they're there. So this is what I aspired to achieve—a type of invisibility—and when I took Justin's sleeping bag home with me that afternoon, I felt like I'd found an eraser for some final part of me that could still be seen.

On the subway, though, I had the sense that everyone was looking at me. They couldn't have known I was holding onto the sleeping bag of a dead man, of course, but I felt that they did. And I kept standing up to stretch my legs, too, afraid that they were clotting.

By the time I emerged into sunlight, I knew I'd never last a whole night in the thing. It was like the bag was haunted.

At home I crammed it into the back of my closet, where it remained, like a hidden reminder of all the world's tragic possibilities, any one of which could, at any moment—poof—just make me disappear.

2.

The second thing happened only a few weeks later, when I was in the apartment of a musician named Ben Lee. He was a songwriter from Australia who'd become somewhat famous when he was young, and then later even more famous when he started dating the actress Claire Danes, who he stayed with for years. I'd owned one of Ben's records before he hired me, which made me feel a little awkward around him, because I'd been a fan, but it was really the fact that Ben's girlfriend was a famous actress that made me feel uncomfortable around him. Not that Claire was ever rude to me. Quite the contrary. She and Ben were both very nice and surprisingly normal. It was just that extra level of celebrity that she brought to the mix that I never quite got used to. I couldn't shake the feeling that, when I was around them, I was nothing more than the help. Which, of course, I was, in a way, but it was surely my own hang-up, not theirs, because if anything, Ben and Claire seemed determined to make the whole band feel like part of the family. We even rehearsed in their Soho apartment, where Claire had her own drum set, and that's what I used. Claire Danes's drum set! One morning I remember she emerged from the bedroom in a white bathrobe and calmly picked up my crossword while I played her drums, working it while we rehearsed. There was fruit on the table.

Coffee. My *New York Times* folded up on a chair. This is what it was like. Very domestic. We practiced right there in the living room, talking about current events between songs.

On the afternoon in question, though, I was over there packing for an out-of-town gig when Ben mentioned we'd be sleeping at a friend's house that night. I'd thought we were staying in a hotel. Not that I cared. It's just that, if I'd known, I would have brought a sleeping bag with me. Not Justin's. I was never sleeping in that thing. I would have just borrowed someone else's. Now, though, I was again in that position I hated: unprepared and conspicuous. It made me feel unprofessional, so I cringed at what I was going to say next. Still, I said it. "I just, I don't have a sleeping bag."

"No problem," Ben said, totally unperturbed. "Just look in the closet. Claire's got all sorts of stuff in there."

The "closet" was a long walk-in space off the living room, which held a tidy collection of luxury shoes, jackets, bags, and umbrellas, each with a surprising amount of space left around it, as if on a display shelf. I had the feeling my chances of finding camping gear in there were slim. But then I saw it in the back—a brand-new, shiny, never-before-used bright yellow sleeping bag, rolled into a bundle with straps.

"Sure she won't mind?" I said, emerging from the closet with it.

"Yeah, no," Ben said. He shrugged. It was obvious he had never laid eyes on the thing.

After the show we drove through the outskirts of town. It was late. One or two in the morning. This was in Northampton,

Massachusetts. Our headlights seemed to get soaked up by the darkness as we slipped through it. The house we reached was odd and shabby, lit by only a few overhead bulbs. I can't remember whose place it was, but the inside was strangely empty, as if someone hadn't yet moved in. My room, like the rest of the house, had almost no furniture in it, just hardwood floors and an amp in the corner. I didn't care. I was tired and there was a floor, so I closed the door behind me and read for a while, coming down from the show, until finally I untied Claire Danes's sleeping bag and tried to figure out how to get into it. This proved harder than expected. I located one large opening, but then a second one appeared on the opposite end and confused me. I inspected further, only to discover two narrow tubes attached to the middle. I held the sleeping bag out at arm's length, trying to wrap my head around what I was holding. And then I realized that Claire Danes's sleeping bag wasn't a sleeping bag at all. It was a giant puffy down coat.

Never before had I seen anything like it. It was like an inflated kimono. And yet it had been rolled up like a sleeping bag! What the hell? I imagined there was some fashion designer somewhere who had given this thing to Claire as a promotion, after which she just tossed it in the back of the closet, because really, who would ever wear a thing like this? Or maybe Claire was planning to wear it. What did I know? I had a shaved head and dressed in plain white T-shirts. This coat looked like it came from a different world completely.

I opened the bedroom door, looking for someone to help, but by now the hallway was dark. It seemed like everyone else was asleep. And the last thing anyone wants is their hired drummer going around in the middle of the night, knocking on doors. So I turned back to the coat.

I spun it around in my hands a few more times, checking to make sure that it really wasn't some type of sleeping bag. It truly had looked just like one when it was rolled up. But no. It was still a giant puffy coat. And then I guess I knew what was going to happen next, because it was chilly and I was in an empty room and had nothing to sleep in: I put on the coat.

The first thing I did was hold out my arms like I was a zombie and walk around the room like that a few times, laughing. Then I stopped and patted myself on the stomach, as if I'd grown fat. Eventually I lay on the floor. I was a little scared of what someone might think if they found me there, but it wasn't enough to keep me awake. After just a few minutes of staring up at the ceiling I closed my eyes and I slept.

In the morning, I awoke before anyone else. Quickly I slipped the coat into its sack, hoping to get it packed up before anyone saw. My guess was that Ben would have thought it was hilarious if I'd told him what the thing really was, but then again, I wasn't so sure. Did the rules about loaning your girlfriend's belongings to your friends change when your girlfriend was somebody famous? I didn't know. It seemed best to say nothing it all.

On the way home we stopped at a small river where Ben stacked rocks in the shallows, in the manner that some followers of an Eastern religion do. Or maybe it's just people who seem like they are into Eastern religions who stack rocks this way. I'm not sure. It's the sort of thing Ben enjoyed, though, so I followed suit, and it felt a little silly but also nice. I imagined I was spiritual. Back in the van, Ben and the bass player, a kind young man with long blond dreadlocks, inspected some crystals inside a Ziploc baggie. Real crystals, not drugs. The kind you might find at any museum gift store. I leaned over to take a look, and Ben handed me one. It was black and about an inch long. While I was trying to imagine what powers this crystal was supposed to have, Ben told me I could keep it. It was a kind gesture, and it softened something inside me. Suddenly I felt the need to share something of my own with him too.

"Claire's sleeping bag was actually just a big weird coat," I said.

"What?" Ben said.

"Yeah. That thing from your closet? I thought it was a sleeping bag but it turned out to be a weird puffy coat."

"What?" He laughed. "Really?"

"Yeah. I slept in it."

"What!? Oh my God, that's funny," he said, and then went back to looking at crystals. "Wow."

He couldn't have cared less. I imagine he forgot the story within seconds. And why shouldn't he have? All I had done was borrow a thing that no one cared about. The story I'd been so scared of telling was simply about a sleepy man inside an empty room wearing an unwanted coat.

3.

The third thing happened during a period when Ben was playing a residency at a bar called the Fez. This meant we performed there every week for a month. I loved residencies because they required no traveling—after every show I could just sleep in my bed. Sleeping bag problems were solved. Celebrity friends of Ben's would come by and sit in with us during the run. Mark Ronson and Karen Elson did some songs, a few actors, even Claire Danes herself played my drums one night while Ben sang Neil Young's "Harvest." It was fun.

The most memorable show for me, though, was when Evan Dando joined us. He was the singer for the Lemonheads, a band I'd been a fan of when I was younger. I'd idolized Evan as a kid (as had Ben, actually, who first came to prominence as a fifteen-year-old after writing a catchy paean to him called "I Wish I Was Him"), so it really wasn't much work for me to learn the songs at all. Already I'd played along to them a few thousand times while wearing headphones in my mother's attic.

The stage at the Fez was small, but Evan was sneaky big (or, as Ben described him in "I Wish I Was Him"—"He's got big biceps and a masculine shout"), so when he stood at the mic he ended up taking up more space than I expected and I found myself scared to hit the crash cymbal because it was so close to his back. Still, I hit it when I needed to, and the songs went well. The graduate teaching assistant from my film class stood near the front row, calling out my name between songs. "Nic!" she said. "Whoooo!"

The last song, "Rudderless," was one that my high school band had played at a pep rally. It felt strange to be performing the real thing with the actual songwriter now, and I thought about the singer of my old band, Mark, and how much he had loved the song. I wished he was there with me that night. The whole situation was sort of messing with my head, actually, so by the time I got to the final chorus, I think I was a little distracted. The last few bars feature a dramatic break where, just before the last note, the whole band stops playing and Evan sings "like a ship without a rudder" by himself in the gap. When we reached the spot, though, and everyone else stopped, I just kept playing. Tore right through the break, at full volume, all by myself. It felt like the worst mistake a sideman could make, as if I'd accidentally knocked a spotlight over so that it shone away from the star and instead directly into my face.

After the show, I found Evan backstage.

"Hey man," I said. "I'm really sorry about missing that break."

Evan looked up at me. There he was. The big handsome guy I had idolized. The man who I had shared a stage with only minutes before, standing so close to me that I was worried about hitting my cymbal. His eyes remained utterly blank as he looked at me now, though. It was clear he had no idea who I was.

I still don't understand exactly what powers crystals are supposed to have, but the one Ben Lee gave me that morning in Massachusetts still lives in my desk drawer. It has the power of staying with me, I guess. And Justin's sleeping bag has stayed with me too. Or so I thought. I just looked for it in the basement, but it's gone. I don't remember what happened to it. I'm not sure Justin was even the guy's name, now that I think about it. I say it aloud—"Justin"—and it sounds strange on the tongue. *Justin.* Who was he? Probably those musicians I played with as a sideman would ask the same of me now. Nic. Who was that guy? Was that even his name? I sat on the stage with them, I played their songs, I recorded their albums, and I guess I did the job well, because even if I made a mistake during one of their choruses or slept in their girlfriend's strange clothes, they still couldn't quite see me. I'd achieved the ultimate goal of the sideman: I'd made myself invisible.

7 | HERE LIES JARED FALCON

Falcon was the name of the band. A silly name, I know, but that was why we chose it. We didn't expect to generate interest. It was a "side project." Not that the band wasn't good—it was the best band I was ever in, I think, though that seems to get lost in the storytelling about it now, because of the other things that came to pass—but at the time it was the one band I worked with that felt purely artistic. All other work was just work. For many years—a good eight straight, from my first major label deal to the time Falcon came together in the early 2000s—I made my living as a drummer. Largely this was with major label bands at a time when major labels still controlled the industry and there was money to be made off them and there was no need to be your own publicist on social media or even worry about anything other than learning the parts and not being crazy. Of all the acts I worked with, though, Falcon is the one that has remained most a part of my life, if only because it helped bring about the end of my career.

Before we get to the end, though, I must recount the band's origin story, because it is remarkable.

Falcon was not a cover band, yet our material was not original. What we played were the never-before-heard songs of a dead child songwriting prodigy. His name was Jared Falcon, and in the mid-eighties, Jared attended Petaluma Junior High in Petaluma, California, where one of his classmates was Shannon Ferguson—later the guitarist for the New York City band Longwave, with whom I played for a time. The legend goes that Jared played baritone saxophone in his middle school orchestra and didn't do very well as a student, but he was an exceptional songwriter, penning a new song almost every day and recording each onto a Fisher-Price tape recorder. This practice started in January 1987 and ended, 336 songs later, in February 1988, when he died from spinal meningitis at age fourteen. Years later, on a visit home, Shannon found Jared's dusty pile of old cassette tapes while helping Jared's mother clean out an old storage space, and he knew at once he'd struck gold. Upon his return to New York, Shannon set out to form the band that would bring Jared Falcon's songs to life. And thus, Falcon was born.

This story, of course, is not true. There was no Jared Falcon. Even his name, to my eyes, is an obvious fake. But after the band booked our first show—at Pianos, on Ludlow on the Lower East Side—the club requested a bio and I was tasked with writing the thing. I was the one, after all, who was taking fiction workshops up at Columbia and spending all my time in rehearsal reading *The New Yorker*. Everyone knew that writing was my thing. But while the stories I was turning in for workshop were still largely failures, I had recently started to find some success writing band biographies for groups around town. These are the who-are-they and where-are-they-from statements that accompany almost anything promotional, from websites to club listings to press releases. You've seen them before. They all look the same. And though I was good at cranking them out, the clichéd nature of the form—here are the many adjectives describing the guitar tone (angular, crunchy, slinky), here are the reasons it is the band's best work yet, this is the unique and cute place where the songs were written, this is why they are special—had quickly grown stale for me. So for Falcon's bio I decided to have some fun. And why not? There was nothing at stake. No one was paying me. The band had no label, no revenue, no fans, no real ambition that I knew of. We were just a side project. So I included our actual names in it, where we were from, and the real groups we had a history of working with, but the rest I made up. The whole Jared Falcon thing? That was a joke. At best, I thought, the bio★ would be posted online and someone might laugh at it. Not for one second did I think anyone would ever actually believe it. Slowly, though, and then very quickly, I came to learn I was wrong.

The first believer I met at Pianos. I was cutting through the crowd on my way to the stage when a hand gripped my shoulder. The hand was connected to a man named Mario, a martial arts instructor who had recently begun to date a friend of mine. I had eaten dinner with Mario not too long before, and during the meal he spoke often about fighting with people. "Fucking him up" was a phrase he used repeatedly. I remember thinking

★ See page 97.

my friend had probably made a poor decision about who to date, but I kept my opinion to myself. I didn't want to get involved, especially with this guy. He seemed like a dangerous meathead, so when I found him holding my shoulder that night at Pianos, I was both scared and surprised. I didn't peg him for liking arty indie rock.

"Nic," he said. "I just want to say that what you're doing is beautiful, man."

"What's that?" I said, still scared of the fact that he was touching me.

"About these *songs*, man. About that kid."

It took me a second to realize what Mario was talking about. That by "that kid," he meant Jared Falcon. The human I had made up.

"Oh," I said, and started to laugh. But then it became clear to me that Mario wasn't joking. I could see it in his eyes: Truly, he believed.

"Oh," I said again, now ceasing my laughter as I tried to figure out just how I was going to tell this guy the truth. All those stories about people he had "fucked up" started coming back to me, though, and I was stunned into a moment of silence. Finally I just said, "Yeah, OK, thanks man," and walked off, terrified of what I had done.

Onstage, I bent down beside our keyboard player, Jeff, who was setting up gear.

"Mario thought the bio was real," I whispered into his ear.

"I know!" Jeff said. "He told me he thought it was beautiful!"

"Me too," I said, and we stared at each other wide-eyed, as if only just then discovering that the toy magic wand we'd been playing with for weeks had been casting real spells the whole time.

In the days that followed, we were all a bit spooked. Some-one had another friend who believed too. There were a few of them, in fact. Neil, our singer, even told us that one person he knew had written a piece for a website called *Gawker* about Falcon having "the most complicated backstory in the world." Still, we all laughed. *Gawker?* Come on. This was 2003—the internet was still something I, for one, didn't take very seriously. When someone told me they had "seen something online," I felt a touch of embarrassment for them, as if they were admit-ting to playing a video game. The possibility of invisibility still remained alive in our world, and in any case, fictional rock and roll backstories were a trick of the trade. Gwar, Alice Cooper, Kiss—all basically cartoon characters. None of the Ramones were named Ramone. David Bowie was never an alien. So our own bit of fiction seemed to carry no stakes with it at all. To us, Falcon was just another entry in the long list of bands with false origin stories.

I heard a compelling piece about this trend once on NPR. It was a report on a band named Delicate Steve. The story was not about Delicate Steve's music—slightly precious instrumen-tal rock—but rather about the band's bio, which was a complete lie dreamed up by the author Chuck Klosterman (about the group having been discovered in the parking lot of a strip mall). Perhaps the most interesting aspect of the report, though, was a digression into a 2006 study in which Michael Beckerman, then chair of the music department at New York University, played a piece of music for an audience inside a German church. Half the audience was told it was the work of a composer who, days after it was written, was sent to a concentration camp and killed. The other half learned only the composer's name. After the performance, the half that had not been told the story of the composer's death thought the music was "sweet, lovely, [and] folksy"; the others felt that this was "one of the great tragic statements of the century."

I wonder now if Falcon's story made us sound different to those who believed. If, as we played our songs that night at Pianos, Mario heard not just the music of four young men in T-shirts up there onstage, but also the ghost of Jared Falcon in the room with us, singing into a Fisher-Price tape recorder. If he did, though, that wasn't my intention. I didn't set out to change the way people experienced our music. All I was trying to do was the one thing I'd been struggling to achieve in the rest of my life, which was to write a story that worked.

The first story I wrote—the first *real* story, not including childhood riffs on knights and superheroes and Dungeons & Dragons–influenced monster destruction—was about a man listening to a cassette tape of himself saying the same word over and over. At the end of the piece, the tape pops out of the deck. We never learn what word the man is saying. The story was called "My Brother's Name Is Carved into My Desk"—a title that had nothing to do with the story content—and I wrote it in Bill Moore's eleventh-grade English class, at the Greensboro Day School in Greensboro, North Carolina. The story wasn't very good, but Mr. Moore was pretty great. He was tall and rangy and had a gray beard even though he wasn't that old and he wore cool glasses and played bass in a blues band and was a graduate of Columbia. I remember him drawing a triangle on the blackboard one afternoon, then covering almost all of it in a sea of chalky ripples. He circled the tip of the triangle, the part rising above the fake water, and explained to us how Hemingway's iceberg principle worked: that you need only see the tip of something to understand all that is hidden beneath. I felt like what he had just shown me was something much larger than the tip of an iceberg, though. I felt he had shown me the tip of a new world.

Mr. Moore made everyone in that class subscribe to *The New Yorker*, explaining that we would be reading the magazine all semester long because it held the country's best writing. He built up the classic myth around the magazine, telling us about its editors, its writers, about the Algonquin Round Table, about William Shawn. We never discussed any of *The New Yorker*'s longer pieces, though. All we did was read The Talk of the Town. This is the section in the front of the magazine that includes brief character profiles, vignettes, and anecdotes about city life. Each is a gem in detail, precision, and economy, and as a professor myself now, I still use them in my own classroom from time to time. It's journalism that is excellent, sharp, and doesn't take itself too seriously (while, of course, taking itself very seriously), so I can see why Mr. Moore found them useful. Aside from their craft, though, what The Talk of the Town really provided for those of us in Mr. Moore's English classroom was a promise of life beyond Greensboro. It was like a map pointing us toward all the parts of the world's iceberg that we couldn't yet see, the huge and important things looming out there, submerged in the depths, just waiting for us to discover them.

Once our student subscription ran out at the end of the semester, though, I was left high and dry. I missed the surface buzz I got from those readings, imagining I was elsewhere and cultured and cosmopolitan. So I began reading James Joyce just to say I was reading James Joyce. I bought a collection of Poe simply because the book was so thick. And one afternoon, when driving along Mendenhall Street in Greensboro on my way to meet my friend Bryce at Cup A Joe on Tate Street, I saw a pile of *New Yorkers* standing on a curb and slammed on my brakes.

This was the summer of 1994, when I was seventeen. I had just shaved my head and left the long ponytail I'd worn for years behind on the floor of my friend's apartment. Even the warm summer air through the open windows of my red Karmann Ghia felt cold against my newly bare scalp. The whole world felt fresh. I was primed to become someone new.

I turned my car around and pulled up beside the discarded *New Yorkers*, which I shoveled onto the sizzling black vinyl passenger seat. The address on the top issue revealed the subscriber to be a man named Bill Morris (ignore the fact that his name is almost identical to that of my English teacher, who also happened to live on the very same street, on the same side of the street, only one block away), and at once I recognized the name. Bill Morris was the only novelist I knew of who lived in Greensboro. He drove a big vintage Cadillac convertible, and I'd seen him around town, driving to be seen. I thought he looked cool. The fact that I was retrieving the reading material of an honest-to-god novelist only confirmed what I had already suspected: that this was the most important magazine in the world.

At home, I stacked Bill Morris's *New Yorkers* to the right of my desk and worked through them all summer long, imagining as I did so that I was a refined man of letters, a man in New York, a writer, perhaps, and one who always turned first to The Talk of the Town.

A week or two after the Falcon show at Pianos, I received a phone call in my apartment. There were no cell phones in my life at this time, so I always answered the phone. It was my prime source of work. The person on the other end was not a musician calling to hire me for a session, though. It was a writer, a man who I will call William. I'd met William a few times in person, but I'd known who he was before that. He'd been a contributing editor at *Rolling Stone* and written two books, neither of which I had read, but both of which were cited as "definitive." He'd also published a profile of a band that I liked in *The New Yorker* recently, and I had read it and thought it was great. So getting a phone call from William was much more exciting for me than any musician. For me, this was a *real* star.

We spoke for a moment or two about nothing. It was just small talk, and I found myself wondering—hoping, really—that perhaps William was calling to invite me to a party. Or maybe he did have work for me, maybe one of the musicians he'd recently profiled needed a drummer. Whatever the reason, the mystery was intoxicating, so when he finally said, "Well, I'm calling because I have good news," the tension became almost unbearable.

"Yes?" I said, on the edge of my junky loveseat.

And then William said something that shot right past my desire for an invitation to a party or a new gig and landed deep, deep within me, in the neediest and most tender parts of my soul. Because what he said next was "*The New Yorker* just green-lighted me to write a Talk of the Town piece about your new band."

I pressed my face against the doorjamb in shock. The Talk of the Town? This was too good to be true.

"Oh my God," I said, in a daze. "But what band?"

This was a period when I was working with several new acts at any one time, so it wasn't quite clear.

"About Falcon," William said. "About that incredible story."

And then time slowed to a halt. I felt each breath as it came in and out of me. I was even aware of my awareness, thinking about how I was thinking about each breath, and about how the silence now stretching out over the phone line was growing longer and longer. It was a moment of great importance in my life, I felt, one where a certain dream had been extended to me, as if on a platter, and yet I could not accept it. Not like this.

"Well . . ." I said, guilt rising within me. I couldn't believe I'd just put this man in such a position. "That story is pretty incredible, huh?"

"What are you saying?" William said.

"I'm saying that that story is *pretty incredible.*"

"Wait." He paused, decoding my message. "Are you saying Jared Falcon isn't real?"

"All I'm saying is that the story is *pretty incredible.*"

"OK, OK," he said. He got it now. "Well, um, what I will say is that *The New Yorker* has excellent fact-checkers, so whatever the truth is, it will come out . . ." I could tell he was thinking out loud here, just trying to find some way to salvage the article, because even for him, a Talk of the Town piece would have been a good assignment.

"Look," he finally said. "Don't say anything else. I still might be able to do this . . . I'll make it part of the story? It could even make it more interesting?" It was like he was talking to himself, as if I weren't there. "I want to come to your show at the Luna Lounge. We'll do an interview beforehand."

"OK," I said, and in a blur we arranged where we would meet.

After we hung up, I sat down in a stupor. Gingerly I touched my forehead. There was an indention on it, left there from when I'd been pressing myself against the doorjamb so firmly. The setting sun had fallen between the two buildings outside the window beside me, and its orange light poured into the room. Guilt still coursed through me, but a growing fear had now joined it as well. Was there an advocacy group for survivors of meningitis that might retaliate after I had so carelessly leveraged their trauma? Or some other offended party, one I didn't yet know of? It all seemed possible, and I was afraid of it. There was another emotion at work in me too, though, and it was stronger than my guilt or my fear. Because despite the wild mess I'd just made, despite the fact I'd lied to the world and unwittingly fooled a man I respected and put all of us in the most uncomfortable of positions imaginable, *The New Yorker* had still just called because of a story I'd written. And it was a story they thought was incredible. So more than anything, what I felt at that moment was pride.

A week or so later, we all met at Max Fish. A large tape recorder rested on the table between us. William sat with his back to a door that was filled with bright light, so his form was only an outline.

"So how'd you meet Jared?" he said, pressing record.

Shannon and Neil gave the answer. They'd agreed beforehand to base all responses on a kid they'd both known growing up, so whatever they'd say would line up. And, incredibly, it seemed to be working. Everything they said sounded true. Still, William knew we were lying, and we knew that he knew we were lying, and so the whole thing proceeded like some type of torture. It lasted only a half hour or so, but it felt much longer than that.

In fear I saw William in the audience later, standing near the front of the stage, and afterward, Abby, my girlfriend, told me she'd talked with him.

"I asked him how the interview had gone," she said, "and he said, 'This is going to ruin my writing career.'"

In the weeks that followed, I checked my mailbox with increasing anxiety. Each new issue of *The New Yorker* arrived like a possible bomb. Still, nothing about us appeared in it. In the meantime, *The Village Voice* ran a short profile ("In the annals of concept records, Brooklyn band Falcon has quite a fantastical doozy . . ."). *Entertainment Weekly* did a small piece in which we were "marvelously dreamy." I performed live on WFMU with another act, and while there the DJ interviewed me—the hired drummer of *another act*—about Jared Falcon. And yes, even NPR—the very station that ran the piece about the existence of fake band biographies—aired a segment about the band's backstory, reporting on how Jared Falcon "managed to write and record more than 300 songs in the late '80s on a shoddy tape recorder. The band has recovered those old tapes," they said, "and plays as a tribute band to an artist whose music never made it past living-room cassettes."

I gave up looking for the Talk of the Town piece, though. Over time it just became clear that it wouldn't happen, and for a long time after that I couldn't even read *The New Yorker*. It was like my actions had sullied its pages. Many times I thought about reaching out to William to apologize for having put him in such an awkward position and ask him what had become of it all, but my guilt remained too potent to act. Not until a decade later, not until I was writing the very first draft of this essay, did I email to ask.

"Didn't write anything," he said. "Didn't even transcribe the interview. The band was unknown, so it wasn't interesting to discuss the hoax."

Hoax. Even now, the word burns.

I didn't set out to mislead. I didn't try to create fake news. I just wrote a story about a dead boy's songs and was surprised when people widely believed it. And though I guess it isn't news that a good story can be hard to resist, maybe the most surprising aspect of this whole fiasco was the story about myself that arose from it. And it was one that I couldn't resist either. In this story, I no longer had to show up to a recording session only to learn that the project was a Christian rock album, or a Lens-Crafters jingle. In this story I no longer had to carry my drums up five flights of stairs every night at three in the morning. In this story I made my own artistic decisions and ceased being only a sideman. Because in this story I was no longer a drummer. What I was was a writer, and that fictional bio about Jared Falcon was my first success.

I didn't quite see it that way then, though. Not exactly. This is only a narrative I'm piecing together now, from my comfortable perch in the future. I didn't know then that I would soon apply to graduate schools for writing and get a fellowship to the one that people said was the best. Or that then, when I moved to Iowa to attend that program, I would be tolling the ultimate death knell for my music career. All I knew was that I had written a story that people found compelling, and because of it I found enough confidence to keep writing more stories, hoping another would click.

When I think about Falcon today, though, what comes to mind most vividly is not how the band marked the end of my music career. Instead what I think of is one specific moment, near the end of my time in New York, when we were all in rehearsal. This was just before I left for Iowa. We were arranging a new song on this day, and during the verses, I wasn't playing a standard rock and roll backbeat, but rather something more orchestral and spare. This was one of the great assets of this band—our arrangements were dynamic, unusual, built around open space. In each measure my whole part was only three sixteenth notes on the floor tom—two short pickup notes leading to the one of the next measure: dah-dah-DUM. Shannon, who was playing bass on the song and attempting to play those notes simultaneously with me, kept inverting the phrase and playing three sixteenth notes trailing *after* the one: DUM-dah-dah-dah. This meant we only played one note together in the middle. As the afternoon continued, Shannon kept struggling to figure it out, shaking his head at the simplicity of the part and the weird mental block keeping him from getting it right, until, for some reason, we had a shared epiphany: His error was not an error at all. The phrase we had accidentally constructed was in fact the most perfect part of all: my notes leading into his, a basic call and response.

I've had creative explosions like this in the past, but never again did I have one as pure or exciting, at least not in my music career. I am a writer now. I work alone. And for the most part, I don't miss playing the drums. But I do miss that moment. I miss the rush of shared recognition, of constructing something beautiful by accident and having it change the course of what we were doing. It was like we had accidentally brought something to life in the room with us and were suddenly hearing it there for the first time, like it had a loud and very weird heartbeat, one that shouldn't have worked but it did, going dah-dah-DUM-dah-dah-dah. This was the part of the song, it seemed to be saying, of all the parts of the song, that was most true. And even though we'd just made it up, pulling it out of thin air without even meaning to, it was impossible not to believe in it.

*FALCON

How many bands form with a finite amount of material? Really, think about it. How many bands form knowing, from the start, what the songs already are, and that there will never be another one? It's a problem tribute bands must often face. But what if the tribute band's songs have never even been heard before?

Enter Falcon.

Falcon is not a tribute band.

Falcon plays all new material.

But . . . Falcon will never write another song. In fact, they never have.

Let me explain. Every Falcon song has already been written by the band's namesake, Jared Falcon. However, Mr. Falcon is not in the band.

From 1986 to '88, Jared Falcon attended Petaluma Junior High in Petaluma, California. He played baritone sax in the orchestra and did not do particularly well in school. However, he was a songwriting prodigy, writing close to a song a day and recording each onto a Fisher-Price tape recorder. This practice started in January 1987 and ended, 336 songs later, in February 1988, when Mr. Falcon died from meningitis at age fourteen.

Luckily for us, however, Jared Falcon's classmates from Petaluma Junior High, Shannon Ferguson and Neil Rosen, have since found those tapes. Both now living in New York City, Neil and Shannon have finally formed the band that will bring these amazing songs to life. Neil (vocals, guitar) and Shannon, who also plays guitar with New York band Longwave (RCA), recruited local drummer Nic Brown (Ben Lee, Eszter Balint, Skeleton Key) and keyboardist Jeff Wiens to form Falcon in the winter of 2003.

"It was easy once they heard the songs," Rosen said of finding band members who hadn't grown up with Jared. "The material really speaks for itself. The other guys were excited about it before I even told them the story behind the songs."

Jared Falcon's dusty pile of cassettes was discovered by Ferguson while helping Mrs. Falcon, still a family friend, clean out a storage space in Petaluma.

"It took me about two seconds to realize I'd found something special," Ferguson said of his first listen.

Surprisingly contemporary while simultaneously alien, it seems impossible for the material to have come from the mind of a fourteen-year-old.

"A lot of the songs are about animals. And many don't have what one might conventionally think of as a chorus, or the standard pop structure," Rosen says about the songs, some of which are barely two minutes long, "but once we arrange [the songs] and bring them to life, they really work. Songs this good have a life of their own."

Determined not to be too precious with the material, Falcon has taken the fragile recordings of a deceased boy with an acoustic guitar and transformed them into fully realized, often epic arrangements. To say the songs "really work" is a rather massive understatement on Rosen's part.

"Look. We've only really worked up about twenty songs," Rosen says. "That leaves more than three hundred, you know. I'm not particularly worried about running out anytime soon."

8 | THE NUMEN OF THIS STORY

It was one little write-up. A paragraph, maybe. Shannon called to tell me about it: *Entertainment Weekly* would be including our band Falcon in a column called Download This. In New York, the news could have been almost forgettable. Every other act I'd been working with had gotten much more attention than this. But I was a graduate student in Iowa now, far far away from the city and my music career, so the prospect of anything about me appearing in a national magazine now—no matter how small— came as welcome proof that I was still also a drummer.

"I'll be back in two years!" is what I'd told everyone before we had left. Abby and I had been in New York for four years at the time—she managing the frame shop of a European art gallery, and me playing drums. We'd made careers for ourselves, careers that at one point had seemed almost impossible, so of course we'd be back. We loved the city. It was only a few days after we'd arrived in Iowa, though, that Abby first said, "You know we're never going back, right?"

We were walking around our new neighborhood when she said this, a shady stretch of historic homes in which we now rented our own tiny two-bedroom house, a structure that felt like a mansion compared to our Hell's Kitchen walk-up. We'd stopped at an old elementary school on the other side of our block, and as I stood atop the multicolored map of the United States painted across the cracked concrete courtyard there, I thought of all the places we'd lived. North Carolina. New York. Now Iowa.

Maybe Abby was right. Maybe we weren't going back. Already it was easy to see how life could be elsewhere, away from the city. Simpler. More in tune with nature. Less expensive. In my mind, though, it didn't really matter where we lived, because even if I was a graduate student writing short stories in Iowa City, I would still just be a drummer who wrote. Soon I'd even have an article in *Entertainment Weekly* to help me prove it.

Classes met once a week, ten of us seated around a table in Jim McPherson's office.

Jim was mysterious and inscrutable, a literary icon so reclusive that the *Chicago Tribune* once described him as "only slightly more gregarious than J. D. Salinger." I didn't know that at the time, though. I didn't even know that he was the first African American to win the Pulitzer Prize for Fiction, or that he was one of the original MacArthur "geniuses." I hadn't done much research about any of this beforehand. All I knew was that I had somehow been given a fellowship to attend the Iowa Writers' Workshop, and so the whole situation had started to feel like an extension of my music career to me—simply another arrangement in which someone else was paying for me to pursue a new art project. So when I met Jim at orientation and found that he reminded me of Pete, my old drum teacher, I decided I'd sign up for Jim's workshop, because when I was young Pete had taught me technique and form and I assumed that's what I'd be getting from Jim.

During class, though, Jim didn't talk about technique or form. Mostly what he did was just listen in silence, watching as we spoke among ourselves about our stories, his eyes shifting back and forth above an unreadable grin. Some days he would simply giggle and say, "OK. Thank you." Twice he played an old recording of an interview he had done with Richard Pryor years before, laughing along quietly as he listened. And then when Jim did speak, it was often abstract or hard to pin down. In particular, he liked to talk about "the numen." This was something he'd bring up after pointing out a complication central to a story—something of great importance, like the love of a mother, or the burden of loss—and then he'd say, "See, now that's the *numen*. That's the life force of this story. *Numen* is Latin. For the life force." Sometimes, though, when we talked about some stories—like mine—the numen wasn't so clear. "What is the numen of this story?" Jim would ask, and the room would grow silent.

Later, standing two deep at the Fox Head, someone would say, "So, Jim talk about the numen again?" People would laugh. Yeah, they'd say. The numen. Ha. Yoda, people called him.

I found myself starting to look up from my keyboard during this time, though, and ask *what is the numen of this story I'm writing?* If I'd been struggling with a drum part, the solution would have been easy—just practice it more or rearrange notes. Asking myself Jim's question, though, didn't solve much at all. If anything, it just made things worse. My stories, it seemed, were about nothing.

Classes. Shortening days. Driving through cornfields, watching the wind move over them like a body of water. When would I start missing the drums?

I'd set them up in our basement. After years of not having enough space to own even a couch, it seemed utterly decadent now to have room for a whole set of drums. Only once did I sit down at them for an extended stretch, though, and that was during a tornado warning, just after dark. The sirens wailed as I descended the stairs to the basement, where I tapped out a few patterns while waiting for danger to pass. Tornadoes in the Midwest. It all seemed sort of funny to me at the time, like an Americana cliché. Dorothy and Oz and all that. So when a train roared past—our house was near some tracks—I found it doubly hilarious, since I'd always heard people say a tornado sounded just like a train.

When I came back upstairs, though, I found one shred of pink insulation lying on our front stoop. More of it dangled from the trees in the yard, like radioactive Spanish moss. The town was dark all around me. That train hadn't been a train at all, I realized. It had been the tornado.

I made some new friends. Three classmates, all a few years older and much more experienced. Matthew had just published a story in *The Paris Review*. Austin already had a book deal and was writing for *The New York Times Magazine*. And Kevin had just finished an assignment for *Harper's*. I, on the other hand, didn't even know that *The Paris Review* wasn't from France. I really thought Matthew was bilingual.

"You've never read Lorrie Moore?" he said to me one night, in a dark booth at George's.

"You don't know Barry Hannah?" Kevin said on a different night, smoking outside the Fox Head.

"Oh man," they would say in disgust. "Oh man." They seemed to relish uncovering my ignorance.

"Here, read this book," they would say, determined to fix me. "Here, here's this story."

I soaked it up. In a way, these guys were providing me with what I'd expected from Jim—the craft notes, the practical advice, the reading lists and the pointers—but while I felt my writing was finally improving at least some with the help of these classmates, Jim's lessons remained largely mysterious. He just kept watching our workshop in silence, listening, giggling from time to time, and coming back to the numen. At times, I found myself wondering if I'd picked the right teacher. Maybe, I thought, Jim wasn't teaching me anything at all.

There was one other musician in Iowa City that I knew of. He was the husband of a classmate, a man almost too handsome to be attractive, and I'd heard he was an aspiring songwriter. I never officially even met this man, yet I grew increasingly and irrationally afraid of him. If I saw him in the grocery store, I'd cut into the next aisle. If he was at a party, I'd avoid him at all costs. I never once let music come up in any conversation anywhere near him or his wife, and yet I'm not sure he even knew who I was—let alone that I played the drums. Nevertheless, I'd still somehow convinced myself if he did find out, he would ask me to play with him, and I did not want to play with him. My last job had been a two-month session in a mansion on top of a mountain where I recorded an arty rock record with Radiohead's producer. The idea of working with an aspiring songwriter in Iowa City held no appeal for me, and while I suppose part of my resistance was that I thought I was too good for the guy—something not fun to admit, but I think probably true—that wasn't the real issue. The main complication for me was that, as a drummer, I'd been yoked to the projects of others for so many years that now, as a writer, I had suddenly become so intoxicated by the opportunity to have an artistic project be all my own that any hour potentially spent working on someone else's art seemed like a waste of my time.

One afternoon, while I was alone in my house, writing, probably thinking about the numen and failing to come up with an answer, I heard a knock at the door. All our new friends lived in the neighborhood, so I assumed it was one of them. Calmly I walked down the hallway. When I opened the door, though, I was shocked to find Jim on the stoop.

"Jim?" I said, looking around. His old Honda was parked at the curb. "Did something happen? You OK?"

"I'm sorry," he said, "but I was just driving by, and I saw that sign . . ."

He pointed to a campaign sign for a local election that was

stuck into a neighbor's yard. It read something like *Bob Dooker for Sheriff.*

"And I thought," he said, "I thought, well, if that guy doesn't win, he's going to be in some deep dooker, isn't he?" And then he burst into laughter. "I'm sorry," he said, clearly not sorry at all. "I'm sorry." He continued to giggle, almost uncontrollably. "I just, I had to tell someone. I'm sorry."

I laughed along politely as Jim pulled himself together, but I couldn't believe what he had said. Had Jim McPherson really just stopped by my house to tell me a joke? I waited for more, but nothing more came. Jim simply said goodbye and shuffled back to his car.

I closed the door and stood there for a second. Jim lived around the corner, so I guess that's how he'd known where I lived, but was that enough reason to stop and tell me a joke? I didn't know. I still don't. Maybe he thought my sense of humor was bad enough that I'd enjoy his little spark of wordplay, which I guess I did. But whatever the reason, after that visit Jim and I began to spend more time together. He invited me and Abby over for dinner. He asked for my help operating his "internet TV," a clunky interface that he used to check his email on his television set. And then one afternoon, he even shared a photocopy with me of an excerpt from an uncompleted writing project of his. So later when he asked if I wanted to start coming with him to a local nursing home to help teach a free weekly writing workshop for the elderly, I said, yeah, of course. I was honored he'd asked.

At the first class, though, only three people showed up. One was a woman who told a story about a house she had lived in as a child. Another spoke of her dolls. And the third told us about some memory problems her husband was having (a story she then proceeded to tell again the very next week). I listened to it all politely but impatiently, waiting for them to share what they'd written. Soon it became clear, though—they hadn't written a thing.

I wanted to scream that Jim was a Pulitzer Prize–winning author here. That they needed to honor his time and actually write something down if we were going to run a writing workshop for them. But Jim didn't seem bothered at all. He just sat there, grinning and listening.

One evening, Abby and I hosted a dinner party. It was the first time we had done something like this. In New York there just wasn't room. Here, though, we had a whole house to fill up with friends. Matthew and Kevin brought their wives and their children. Austin brought his boyfriend. We ate in the living room in front of our remote-controlled fireplace and then moved to the tiny backyard, where beneath a string of lights we drank cheap beer. The leaves had all changed. There was a nip in the air. Intermittently a car would woosh past, but otherwise the neighborhood was silent. Around us our new friends talked about books. Children played in the lawn. I felt a shift taking place in my world, along with the seasons.

Then somebody said it: "So, Nic, your drums set up?"

I guess I'd been expecting it. They knew about my career. I'd even burned off some Falcon CDs for them when we first arrived, relishing the chance to edit my musical identity down to the one project I loved most of all. Still, as I followed my new friends down to the basement, I was surprised to feel a growing sense of dread.

It had been years since I'd attempted to entertain anyone with just drums alone. For me, the idea of musical performance was all tied up with the band. By myself, I had no idea what to play. Thud. Crack. Boom. I just moved through the kit like this, drum by drum, dully, until finally deciding on a sixteenth note pattern I'd performed with a songwriter not too long before, a funky little part lifted off an old R&B record. As soon as I started to play it, though, all the groove I remembered was gone. Without the guitar, without the slinky bass line playing along with me, the notes were just drums in a basement. After only a few measures, I hit my cymbal and stopped.

Everyone continued to stare at me.

"Is that it?" someone said.

"Well, yeah," I said. "I mean, no one wants to hear drums by themselves."

And then the people who had just asked to hear me play the drums by themselves followed me back up the stairs, and we never spoke of it again.

Fall hardened to winter. I would see my drums when I went to the basement for laundry, but that was about it. All my energy was directed toward my writing now, and with the nights growing longer, I started going to sleep early and waking before dawn. Those early hours were like visiting a new wing of a house. I recognized the world through the windows, yet everything around me felt different. Headlights passed slowly along the street, illuminating small hedges of snow. A few walkers passed by, dogs at the end of a leash. The paper, thudding onto the walk. Mostly, though, the hours were empty. They were mine, and in them I wrote.

What I would do is finish a new story, take it to the Dey House, and run off twenty-five copies. Then I'd seal each into a manila envelope addressed to one of the literary journals I'd found listed in the back of the previous year's *Best American Short Stories*. It sounds so old-fashioned now, but at the time—2004— it felt like the only way to take the first step into a new career. All I wanted was someone at one of these places to say that they'd publish something by me, anything, just to prove I was more than a drummer playacting the part of an author. According to the editors of these journals, though, my stories were "unusual." Or they were "promising." Or they were something that they wanted to "see more of." Invariably, though, they were not something they wanted to publish. "Thank you for your submission," the photocopied rejections would say. "But this does not suit our needs at this time."

In the meantime, some of my classmates were showing up in *The New Yorker*. A few were already signing book deals. And one in particular, a student from China, was drawing huge national attention for stories she was writing that all felt important and big. I thought of her as Jim's other "student friend"—he was close to her too—but I imagined that when she asked herself what the numen of her stories was, she could come up with answers.

I still felt a cold emptiness when asking Jim's question of my work, though. What *was* the numen of my stories? Nothing nothing nothing. And what did I have to write about? Compared to my classmate—the one from China, whose life experiences already included new motherhood and cross-continental immigration—my own life seemed barren of import. So finally one day I just stopped thinking about myself and started to imagine the life of someone else. In particular, one of those women who attended the weekly writing workshops in that nursing home with Jim. Already I'd learned so much about their lives that it wasn't too hard to conjure one up, and so now, at my keyboard, I asked myself what it was that might keep a person like that returning to a writing workshop in which no one ever wrote. Loneliness? A desire for connection? A deep longing for some type of companionship? So I wrote about those things, wrapping them into an elderly character named Evelyn. The story ended with Evelyn holding on to a stray dog, after having just saved him from choking on a piece of meat, thrilled at the brief connection to that strange panting life.

After reading it Jim nodded silently to me at workshop, pursing his lips, and only a few weeks later I got a note from the *South Carolina Review* saying that they'd accept it, contingent on a few edits. I held on to that slip of paper for several long moments. Then I hid it. I knew at once I wouldn't tell anyone. Not at first. Because the letter wasn't even an outright acceptance, and yet it was embarrassing to me just how important it felt.

My story about Evelyn wasn't the best story in the world. It was fine. But it was a breakthrough for me, and I think the real difference between it and the ones I'd been writing before was that I'd found a way to get out of my own head and start thinking about the importance of others. And all that time I'd thought Jim wasn't teaching me anything at all. What I realize now, though, is that Jim's workshops—those in his office, but even more so those in the nursing home—weren't supposed to be about technique and form. We could learn about that stuff anywhere. What Jim was trying to teach us was something bigger, and less easy to define, and if I had to put a name on it I think I'd call it empathy. At the time, it was probably the lesson I needed most.

When the issue of *Entertainment Weekly* with Falcon in it was finally published, I told Abby I needed to buy some dish gloves at the Hy-Vee. I was embarrassed to admit I was really just going to pick up a copy of *Entertainment Weekly*. What I found on the magazine rack, though, was a few lines about my band, and even a photo of Shannon and Neil along with it, but nothing about me on the page. Not even my name.

People rattled past with their carts. It made sense, I told myself, as I closed the magazine slowly. I lived in Iowa now, so how could I have been at the photo shoot? And why mention me as a member of the band when I'd moved so far away that I couldn't even play with them? Still, my absence came as a shock, and as I stood there, coming to terms with what it might mean, I thought back to what Abby had said just after our arrival in Iowa, about how we'd never be going back to New York. She must have already known what was only just starting to become clear to me. And my band members had surely understood it too, and even my new friends in town. But not me. Not yet. Not until that moment, standing there in the aisle at the Hy-Vee, did it occur to me that what I'd done by moving to Iowa wasn't just move to Iowa. What I'd done was quit playing the drums.

In the parking lot I sat in the car for a while. The sky was gray. It was cold. Sometimes, during those days, the temperature would fall ten degrees below zero, and yet I never wore more than Adidas Sambas with thin cotton socks. I slept under two meager blankets at night, clutching them close to my chest in the dark. And I owned just one warm coat, a wool packer that I wore over nothing more than a T-shirt. It was like I didn't even know it was cold, as if I were somewhere else completely, outside my own body, looking around, unaware of what I was feeling.

I suppose I started the car after a while and then drove it home, where I would have washed the dishes with my old dish gloves, since I'd forgotten to buy new ones as cover. Surely I would have then gone to sleep early and awoken before dawn, because already that was my writing schedule, and if this was a story I was writing in those predawn hours back then, I might even have asked myself what the numen of this story was. And the answer, for once, would have been clear: This was a story about a man who'd changed the course of his life, and the moment he finally knew it.

SNARE DRUM

Ludwig, brass. Limited edition. Good condition. Tube lugs. Received as a Christmas gift from my mother in 1995. In recent years it has been set up in my daughter's bedroom, where we like to lie on the floor beneath it and hum loud enough to make the snares rattle. *Aaaaah*, we say and then laugh. *Aaaaaaaaaaaaaaaah*. Brush wear visible on head. 14" x 5.5"

MARCHING BASS DRUM

Slingerland. Circa 1920. Wood. Purchased in Kansas City from an antique store where it was being sold for decorative purposes. Price: $75. Original calfskin heads played until broken. Too big for storage, it hung on the wall in my New York City apartment for years, where I used it as a sock drawer. I'd dump out the socks before playing a show, but during performances I'd often find one was still in there, bouncing around. 26"

SNARE DRUM

Ludwig, circa 1965. Wood. Silver sparkle finish. Fair condition. Missing strainer. A label reading "Jive Nipple" is affixed to the shell, placed there during a 1996 recording session at Overdub Lane in Durham, North Carolina. Meaning of phrase lost to time. Original owner Peter Hicks, middle school friend. On the last day of tenth grade, while cleaning out a storage room, the band teacher asked if anyone knew who the drum belonged to. I said it was Peter's. Peter had stopped attending Greensboro Day School years ago, though, so I offered to take it home and return it to him. It has remained in my possession since. 14" x 5.5"

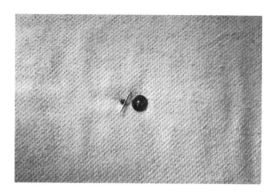

CYMBAL AND DRUMSTICKS LAPEL PINS

Good condition. Given as a gag gift in 2004 by Steve Schiltz, singer of the band Longwave, with whom I was playing. Worn once, the night I received them, on the pocket of a Wrangler jean jacket. Stored in my desk drawer ever since, where they appear every few years while I am hunting for paper clips.

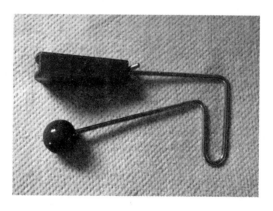

VIBRASLAP

LP. Very good condition. Produces hilarious rattling sound effect. Kept on mantel in living room where I argue it resembles modern sculpture. Striking it on any surprise downbeat creates immediate surge in "wacky" feelings. Excellent for use during family dance parties.

DRUM SET

Gretsch. Circa 1970. Fair condition. Champagne sparkle. Purchased in Los Angeles in 1997, after finding an advertisement in the newspaper. Price $250, which took me two days to remove from an ATM machine, since my account at the time had a $200-a-day cap. Hoops and hardware replaced. 22", 13", and 16"

BRASS BELL

Asian? Good condition. A gift from the owner of Harvey West Music in Greensboro, North Carolina. Given to me in 1987, when I was ten, after I had taken it off a display rack of assorted noisemakers and admired it while my mother paid for some drumsticks. "You can have that, if you want," the owner said. "Really?" I said. He smiled and nodded. The bell produces an almost inaudible clank and has never been "played" as part of any musical event. It hangs from the corner of a framed watercolor on the wall beside my bed.

HI-HAT CYMBALS

Sabian. Hand-hammered. Provided for free by Sabian in 1997, after I broke my own cymbals and called management to say I needed new ones but did not have the money. Management arranged for a Sabian endorsement. I kept the cymbals but declined the endorsement, preferring Zildjian instead. Despite disliking both the sound and the weight of the cymbals, I have used them exclusively since. When I play them, I still think, *I need to buy a pair of Zildjians.* 14"

CYMBAL BAG

Make unknown. Very poor condition. Heavy use. Duct tape reinforcement at bottom. Total failure of Velcro enclosure at top. American Tourister luggage label taken from Samsonite suitcase purchased at PTA Thrift in Chapel Hill. Label reads: NIC BROWN 416 W 56th Street #20 New York, NY 10019 212.957.2779. Bag acquired in 1989, so that I could carry my cymbals to UNCG band camp. Two other cymbal cases have been purchased over the years, but this one, a cheap no-name model, is the one I've always used.

DRUMSTICK BAG

"BIG" by LP. Poor condition. Heavy use. Signs of seam repair. Broken zipper pulls replaced with zip ties. Originally owned by legendary jazz drummer Max Roach, who left it behind after a performance on the campus of UNCG in 1996. My roommate at the time, Chuck, was a student employee and found the bag. Outreach to Roach's management company resulted in no response, after which Chuck gifted it to me for my nineteenth birthday. Another student had taken out all the drumsticks. All that remained were three toothpicks, each slightly chewed.

10 | SLEEP

Providence. Omaha. Peoria. Toronto. I can look at a map, pick out almost any town, and tell you I've been there. But I haven't, really. I've only been to the club. There was never enough time to see much more than that. And the shows themselves, they all blur together. It was like we were just driving around the same town every day, cutting back in after dark to find a new theater. What details do linger, though, after all those years, are the hours I spent around sleep. The surprise of each night's bed. The winding down. The fading away. The waking and the light in the morning. This is the region of magic. These are the things I remember.

I sleep on the couch of a beautiful high school classmate of my older brother. She's in college now and we've come to her town. I awake before anyone else and step onto the porch. A small Christmas parade is moving past in the street. I can't believe it.

Why is a parade happening at this hour? I wave to Santa as he passes and he waves back, almost as if in slow motion. I could find that house again right now, if we were to go back. I could point you to the exact spot on the street where I parked.

I sleep in the backseat of Gill's Plymouth Valiant, the light coming early.

I sleep in the passenger seat of my red Karmann Ghia.

I sleep on a pale futon in the back of the van. Everyone else is inside. The light from the parking lot through the windows. The sound of the highway like waves in the distance. The surprise cold of a summer night in northern Colorado.

I sleep with my head on the window. We're in the Midwest now, driving. It's early afternoon. I open my eyes and am surprised to see a man being chased across a cornfield by two policemen on foot. The fugitive is far ahead. The field is enormous, and the police are not gaining ground. The space between them just stays the same as they run. It's like the chase could go on forever. The men grow smaller and smaller until eventually we pass out of view. I wonder what happened to that guy. If they caught him. I go back to sleep.

I sleep on the couch in my high school girlfriend's apartment in D.C.

I sleep at the house of a crew member's mother. There is great fanfare about who gets which room. This one's for you. And this one for you. And so on. I am shown to a guest room decorated in early 1980s grandmother style. There is much frill and flowery wallpaper. I thank our hosts profusely and close the door, but then when I pull back the covers I discover some type of insect has laid its eggs in the sheets. Worms are crawling all around in there. I'm not sure what to do. I look at the door. I don't want to offend anyone, though, so carefully I just remake the bed and lie on the floor.

Floors. So many floors.

I sleep on my back with my arms crossed over my chest like a vampire.

I sleep with wax earplugs.

Only every now and then do I roll over and find that my hip bone has become sore from the floor. It'll have a bruise on it later, just one little dot. Otherwise, I sleep well on a floor. Floors are just fine.

I sleep in motels. So many motels. I find a used diaper under the bed of one and it doesn't bother me. Someone says, "Hey man, there's an old diaper under there," and I just leave it.

For years we sleep five to a room. We can't afford more. The guys think I'm taking one for the team when I sleep in the van, but the truth is I like it better out there. I prefer the solitude. One night I'm in the motel, though. Maybe the van's in a deck. We sleep two to a bed at the time, and Mark takes the other side of mine on this night. I dream about my girlfriend while I sleep and then later wake to Mark laughing. "Nic," he's saying. "Nic. Hey." I open my eyes. I've draped an arm over him.

One day, while driving, we get word on the cell phone— the only one we have, the one that our road manager carries on his belt in a holster—that that night's show has been canceled. It is like we've been given a snow day. We're giddy and almost immediately pull off at a lime green motel built into a hillside. Nothing else is around. Maybe this is in Kentucky. Somewhere hilly and lush. For some reason, we get our own rooms—a rarity—and I lie on the bed in mine, feeling like a great expanse of time has just been discovered, almost as if there was an extra day we had found on the calendar, one whose existence had never been known. I feel wonderful. I don't listen to any music on my headphones. I don't make any long-distance calls. I just turn on the motel TV and find the movie *Multiplicity* starring Michael Keaton, a movie which is mediocre and confusing, but which I watch till the end. The daylight remains bright until late, a greenish yellow glow that seems to expand through the windows. I leave the door open, as if the light is fresh air that I'm letting in. We walk to a gas station near the exit later and buy a few beers. The parking lot has a couple lights that rattle and buzz. After dark I sit on the balcony with my legs dangling off, drinking a beer with George, the guy who sells our T-shirts. I sleep deeply that night.

I sleep on the tour bus.

I sleep on an airplane, easily. I like the feel of not knowing what city we're flying to.

I sleep in the luxury suite for the lead singer of another band one night. This is in New York City. It's winter, and cold. The singer has been moved to a different room because the heater in this one has broken, but I heard them talking about it earlier, about how big the room was, and so later when I find the door propped open I walk in. The space is indeed immense. It takes up a whole corner of the building. I've never slept in a room like this before, so I crawl under the mounds of luxurious bedding and imagine what it might be like. It's warm under there, under all those blankets, and so I stay put. Eventually I fall asleep. When I awake the windows are crusted in ice. I lay there for a long time, watching that ice glimmer in the early morning light. Then when I get out of the bed I start shaking.

I sleep on the top storage shelf backstage at Brownies.

I sleep I sleep I sleep.

And then when we come home, I sleep in my own bed for the first night in months. My friend Chip climbs in through my open window and wakes me, but I go back to sleep. The fax machine on the desk beside my bed wakes me up by cranking out some sheet music for the Canadian national anthem, which we're supposed to learn because we are due to play at some NHL game. I go back to sleep. An old history teacher of mine calls to say she saw me in *Rolling Stone*. I let her leave a message and go back to sleep.

I sleep in Penn Station, my cymbal case strapped to my leg with my belt.

I sleep through takeoff.

I sleep through wake-up calls.

I sleep I sleep I sleep.

In recent years, though, my sleeping has changed.

I went on a road trip by myself not too long ago.

I'll just find a place off the highway, I said to my wife. I don't need anything fancy.

After dark I stopped at an Econo Lodge. The room smelled like an ashtray. The bed felt like a sack of old paperbacks. I lay awake on it for hours, in brief moments drifting away, but nothing I'd really call sleep. Finally before dawn I just got up and made coffee. The coffee tasted like cinders. I sat in the half light at the small desk, sipping it like it was medicine.

Sometimes, I can't even sleep in my own bed these days.

Back then, though, when I was a musician, when I was so busy I didn't even know what town I was in, I never had a night's sleep that was bad. I slept like it was just another leg of my journey, the part I did not want to end.

11 | AN ECLIPSE

The sun bore down on me, hot and heavy and bright. A few wisps of cloud floated around the horizon, but they were far away. The day was so clear that it felt made to be seen, and yet I was not admiring it. What I was doing was standing in my front yard with my head inside a cardboard box, a green bedsheet wrapped around my neck like a giant's scarf.

I was supposed to be looking at the start of the total eclipse of the sun in there, but what I was really doing was marveling at the phenomenon of pinhole projection, because right in front of my eyes I could see the whole neighborhood wobbling around upside down, all because I'd poked a hole in the box with a screwdriver. Incredible! But also very, very hot. So I took the thing off my head, glanced up at what was left of the sun through my 1950s-style sci-fi certified solar eclipse glasses, and went back inside.

An eclipse on August 21? I wasn't impressed. It was going to take a lot more to make this day more special in our house.

Nine years earlier, on August 21, 2008, I'd been living in Chapel Hill and working as an administrator at an art museum, a job that paid me in money, but otherwise left much to be desired. My once-successful career as a drummer was years behind me, and the dream I'd been cultivating in place of it—to be a writer—had hit a long skid. I'd been waking at five to write ever since grad school, but there was little to show for it. I'd placed a few stories here and there, found an agent, and finished a book, but the manuscript had been rejected by every publisher who had read it, and in the meantime the copy I was cranking out at work was so consistently rejected by my boss that I'd began to mistrust my ability to write a sentence, let alone a whole book. "This is a teachable moment," she would say to me, over and over, as she tore apart every page I brought to her desk, but I didn't feel like she was teaching me anything other than how to hate work. So after years of being spoiled by my success as a drummer, it now felt as if I'd entered an eclipse of my own. That life as an artist was over. I would plug away at it. Things might come together. In the meantime I packed my hopes away, as if burying an ember in ash.

So when Abby became pregnant in late 2007, I found myself both elated and scared. I knew I needed something like this to jump-start my life. And while I didn't understand just how much a child would indeed transform my days—making them so much less about myself, and in turn so much better—I was excited about the promise of change.

Then she went into labor, and on August 21, while she sat quietly moaning on our living room couch—amid a thirty-six-hour marathon from which I'm still recovering, even though

I wasn't the one who did any work—my agent called with the news I'd been offered a publishing deal.

"That's great," I whispered into the phone. "But listen, I'm going to have to call you back."

It was the one moment in my life that something more important than a publishing deal was happening to me, an amazing convergence of events that seemed to hold within it some cosmic lesson, as if the world was agreeing to fulfill my selfish desires only once I could recognize how unimportant they were. Or maybe it was all a coincidence. Regardless, only a few hours before I had been a childless ex-drummer with an unpublished book and a job that I hated, but on August 21, I became the two things that now define me most: a father and an author. So in this way, August 21 became a birthday not only for my daughter, but for me as well. A rebirthday. It was the day the sun came back out.

Inside, my daughter, Frances, opened her presents. Outside the moon continued to inch between us and the sun. From time to time we stepped outside to look. What I saw isn't news, but I'll tell you about it anyway—the sun kept going away. It was like every partial eclipse I'd seen before, all of which had been disappointing.

Gradually, though, the world through the windows started to change. The light took on a quality I had never seen before—a bronze, as if filtered through tea. Presents were left on the floor, the wrapping paper wadded in mounds, as we gathered out in the street. The sun was a shimmering toenail clipping above us, and then less than a toenail clipping, and then, as every news broadcast for months had promised, it went away completely.

Abby began to scream.

Frances started bouncing.

My sister-in-law yelled "Mama!"—a name I'd never before heard her use.

And I kept yelling "Look!" as if no one was looking. "Look! Look! Look!"

Yet there was no reason for our surprise. The sun had just done what everyone had said that it would. I didn't understand how dark it would actually become, though. Or what a 360-degree sunset might really look like. Or that bats would fly. Or that the cicadas would sing—and that I would *hear* them singing, that I would *notice*, that nothing would be more obvious. That the quality of the light would be neither the darkness of night nor the dim sun of wildfire smoke. That it would become its own special theater, never before seen by me on this planet. None of this was why the eclipse was special, though. These are all just trappings around the thing itself, like looking at a trophy after triumph. I can't touch the thing itself—the magic as elusive as the orb that floats around in your vision after looking at the sun.

In frustration, I thought, I'll never be able to explain this to anyone. I felt sorry for those who had been outside what they called "the path of totality"—the seventy-mile-wide strip stretching from Newport, Oregon, to Charleston, South Carolina, through which the moon's shadow blocked out the sun completely—especially those who were close to the edge of it, because I could just imagine them thinking that what they'd seen was basically the same as what I had. But now I knew that the difference between a partial eclipse and totality was like the gap between watching someone swim and jumping into the deep end yourself.

For a little over two minutes we screamed and we pointed and we demanded that everyone look, and then a sliver of the sun reemerged and I could have sworn that only twenty seconds had passed. I felt tears in my eyes. It was over too soon! I wanted it back! But it wasn't coming back, at least not until May 11, 2078, the next time another total solar eclipse will pass over my yard, at which point I will be either 101 years old or dead.

At bedtime that night, my daughter and I lay on her mattress together.

"I just can't stop thinking about the eclipse," she said. "I feel like someone *arranged* for it to be on my birthday."

"I know," I said.

"That's the best day I've ever . . ." She searched for the word. "Lived."

I knew what she meant. I'd had one of those days nine years earlier, the day she was born and I learned that my books would be published—the day my own eclipse came to an end, that dark stretch of life when I felt all my hopes had been dashed. And then years before that, I'd had another best day too, on the cold night we learned about our first offer for a recording contract, when I felt all my dreams had come true. But do I really care that much about dreams? I'm not sure that I do, because I don't miss playing the drums much at all these days, and I fear that if pressed, I wouldn't miss writing much either, if for some reason it disappeared from my life. My daughter is different, though. Her childhood is the eclipse I truly don't want to end.

Planets keep spinning, though. They flip day to night. And with every August 21 that comes around my daughter keeps getting older. I have no lingering concerns about appreciating my music career while I had it. I wrung a fair amount of pleasure out of it when it was happening and knew that I had it good. And I feel pretty certain I have a grasp on how lucky I am to have made a life for myself as a writer as well. I'm much less confident about my perspective on my life as a father, though. I just keep wondering how many more days like this one I'll have—a best day, as my daughter described it—before she'll be grown. And if, by then, her childhood will have passed by me completely before I even know how best to appreciate it. I'll just be a man looking around for something that's gone by that point, like I was after the solar eclipse: a guy simply standing there, amazed, wishing it all would come back.

I purchased solar eclipse stamps at the post office a few days later and the woman behind the counter said, "Did you *see it?*"

"It was incredible," I said, almost whispering. "It was so much better than I expected."

"*Me too,*" she said.

I got goose bumps just standing there.

"The eclipse is my god," Abby announced mysteriously at dinner a few nights after that. We all kept eating in silence. No questions were asked.

And then a week or so later, I stepped outside and found my cardboard box lying there, the one with the pinhole in it, neglected beside our front steps. I put it back over my head and looked around, trying to find something exciting. I wondered what the neighbors thought. A man in his yard, alone, his head inside a cardboard box. What had happened to me? The eclipse came to us for only two minutes, but—like my daughter's fleeting childhood, like our memories of joy—something permanent has remained.

12 | IN TENNIS, LOVE MEANS NOTHING

Across the net, Tripp Phillips steps up to the line. He's thirty-two years old, six foot one, and something about him—equal parts confidence, clothing, posture, and tan—communicates the few thousand hours he's spent striking tennis balls perfectly from out of the air. It's like how when you meet someone who's rich, you can just tell they have money. With Tripp, you can tell he has *tennis*. He glances up through a shock of blond hair, places his toss three feet above his left shoulder, and swings.

Tripp holds two ATP doubles titles: Tokyo 2006 and Indianapolis 2008. He's a 2006 US Open semifinalist in doubles. A few years back he peaked at 29 in the world, and this summer—2010—he'll play as Anna Kournikova's partner on a national exhibition tour.

I, on the other hand, played my first and only tournament in 1984 at age seven. There were two entrants—me and my best friend Ralph Brabham—and I came in second.

Today, though, I'm the one on the other side of the net,

bouncing from foot to foot, because this isn't an international tennis tournament. This is a blue court inside a mostly empty tennis center in Chapel Hill, North Carolina, and Tripp is playing me.

I should say here that Tripp is a friend. We met in the nineties, back when we were both in our twenties and living in Chapel Hill. We were ascendent then, he a rising tennis star, and me with a song on the charts. The world was ours. I remember one night, sitting on a front lawn together somewhere, several beers in, proclaiming that we—the musicians and athletes of the world—were the knights and the cowboys of today! That we held the dreams of the youth! Us! It's an embarrassing memory, obviously, but the point is we've known each other forever, so the idea of us ending up on a court together isn't unthinkable. Tripp's hit with me before. Humored me. But never before have we played, because what would have been the point? I've seen him beat Michael Chang at Forest Hills; I've followed his results on Centre Court at Wimbledon. I'd be a waste of his time.

Still, here we are, on a court in the midst of a match, because even though I remain a waste of Tripp's time, and even though he is still a world-class athlete, something about me has changed. I've quit playing the drums is what it is, and ever since I've found a strange void in my life, one I didn't expect, and I think I've been trying to fill it with tennis.

Growing up, I was not an athlete. I was into Dizzy Gillespie and books about orcs. Among my friends—the percussion section of the Greensboro Youth Symphony, the theater kids, the Greensboro skateboarders—sports existed so far outside our circle that they seemed almost exotic. Tennis, though—that was the one I'd always been sort of into. I'd played when I was a kid, after all, and been almost good for a while. So when I met Tripp, I fell back into it easily. He had all these stories about why so-and-so had just lost a match because of staying up all night with a ball girl, or how the hotel rooms in Russia were filled with mosquitos. I'd follow his results online and then get a phone call that night about how the chair umpire was making bad calls. It was intoxicating. Music, on the other hand, had gotten all mixed up with the complications of work for me. I found myself unable to even listen to records that had once brought me joy without now becoming a critic, endlessly parsing style and technique. So tennis became an escape for me, one free of all that, especially since I knew I could never do what Tripp was doing. And why would I want to? He had his tennis, I had the drums.

Once my focus shifted away from drumming, it was around the same time that Tripp scaled back on his own touring schedule and took a coaching position at UNC. We both ended up back in Chapel Hill, got married, had kids. It was a type of afterlife we were living. But Tripp truly transformed his skill set into a new livelihood—coaching and intermittent touring—while I left mine behind completely.

I didn't miss it, though. In fact, I was often amazed at just how little I missed playing the drums. I was fully absorbed by writing now, and the hours I'd once spent hauling gear or rehearsing were consumed with my new book. At the same time, though, something strange started happening to me. The longer

I spent away from the drums, the more I felt compelled to drive down to this one forlorn public tennis court in my neighborhood and hit serves on it all by myself. Or sometimes I wouldn't even serve. I'd just stand there looking around. Eventually I convinced a neighbor to come down and hit with me, but it didn't take long before I started calling the guy so often that I embarrassed myself. It was like I was some eight-year-old, begging him to come out and play.

My obsession didn't make a whole lot of sense. It wasn't like I was very good. But I was getting better, and my awareness of this development was incredibly satisfying. The repetitive practice it required, and the focus on technical minutiae—like a change in grip here, or a shift in the angle of striking—it was all so similar to how I'd learned to play drums. And even the verb was the same: to *play*. So while I didn't miss drumming, I think there were things drumming had brought into my life that I was missing, like the physicality of it, and the demand for mechanical perfection, and above all the need to find someone else to perform with.

As a musician, though, I'd been young. I'd been promising. I'd achieved success and made a career out of it. None of these things would happen for me with tennis. I understood that. Still, I kept playing.

Tripp laughed at my efforts. He made fun of my form. But he also offered pointers from time to time, and after a while— once I started beating my neighbor with some regularity—the question that haunts all weekend warriors popped into my head: How would I really stack up? What would it be like to play a true pro? Unlike most people, though, I had a pro on my speed dial. So finally I just asked him—would he play me in a real best-of-three match, on a sanctioned court, before a live crowd? When he agreed, though, I had no illusions about what was going to happen. He would undoubtedly beat me.

Still, in the days leading up to the match, he talked a whole bunch of trash.

"You are my enemy," he told me over the phone five days before we were to play.

"I am Ivan Drago and you are Apollo Creed. I must kill you," he said three days later.

"I just watched a pillow fight to mentally prepare for playing you," he texted me an hour and a half before the match started.

And even my mother got in on the action. "Wear a helmet," she said, once she learned what I was doing. "One with a facemask."

When we met at the net to shake hands, though, Tripp was all business. He leaned in and smiled, completely at ease. It was like he'd arrived at the office.

"OK. What do you want me to do?" he said. "You want me to hit a bunch of crowd pleasers? Big winners? That'll up my mistakes. Or you want me to play so I win every point?"

I looked at the small group of friends who had gathered to watch. Someone had even brought a bottle of champagne. I considered Tripp's question, but it didn't take long. I didn't come here for anything less than the ultimate test.

"Every point," I said.

The ball has now spun off Tripp's racket and is shooting through the air toward me. It's the middle of the first set, and thus far, here's what I've learned about playing a professional: I can actually trade groundstrokes with him. I can return his serve. I can run balls down for longer than I would have expected. But of the many things that separate me and Tripp, there is one that stands above all the rest, and it's an important one: What I can't do, no matter what, is win one single point.

"It's because you have no weapons," Tripp tells me two days later, over a lunch of cheap tacos. He reviews the match in this specific analytical manner that I've heard him use before, like an engineer inspecting a bridge. "No matter what," he says, "I was going to have you off-balance. And no matter what you did, I was going to be perfectly balanced. I knew where you were going to hit it before you hit it. It's the difference between me and you. But if I played Roger Federer right now, he'd do the exact same thing to me."

Tripp is right about my balance. He just keeps placing the ball where—even if I get to it—I'm so compromised that my legs are jelly and, if I do manage to return it, the ball just lilts over the net. Still, I have one thing working in my favor, which is that the whole match is so ridiculous, and I'm such an over-whelming underdog, that Tripp is a little on edge.

"I'm never nervous during a real match," he says to me later, but on this day, especially since he's agreed to try to win every point, each stroke has become a potential downfall for him. One error and he'll look like he's cracked. I, on the other hand, need only score one point to claim some sort of victory, and the crowd—a dozen adults and four kids under five—is determined to help. They boo Tripp after winners. They heckle him. "Why were you only All-American for one year?" someone shouts. "Didn't you triple double fault once?" says another. None of it seems to faze him, though, and when someone finally does cheer for Tripp after one point (his wife, I see, when I glance up), I'm strangely flattered.

But back to his serve, which is nearing the net.

For almost the whole match, I've been standing so far back that the cinderblock wall is closer to my feet than the baseline, all to compensate for the huge topspin that I know is going to make Tripp's serve jump. But now I step forward. Because I'm going to try something new.

This serve of Tripp's—the one that has just cleared the net cord and now entered the humid airspace above my side of the court—is a second serve, so I know it's returnable, because he's been playing it safe with the pace, making sure he doesn't give me a freebie on a double fault. He guesses they're dropping in around 95 miles per hour, which is slower than he'd hit them in any real match. (My first serves, on the other hand—of which I am rather proud—aren't even 75 mph.) And while Tripp does hit two aces around 120 mph, which seem more like bullets than balls shooting past, the speed in general is something I've managed to adjust to.

When the ball strikes the court, the topspin Tripp has put on it sends it jumping high to my right shoulder, almost as if it's riding an invisible ramp. Instead of taking a full swipe at it, though—which I've been doing with little success—I just sort of chop at it this time, slicing a cute little floater deep into the service box—the last place I want it to land. Because it's going to bounce high and sit up and give Tripp as much time as he needs to rip it anywhere that he wants. But it's also going to give me that one extra second I need to put myself into some sort of position other than desperate defense. And that's something I haven't yet achieved. So as the ball rises before me, I charge the net behind it like I'm fleeing a swarm of angry wasps.

Tripp calmly approaches, covering thirty-nine feet in two seconds like it's nothing, and steps wide to open his forehand, which—as I close into position at the net—he proceeds to hit as hard as he can at my chest. This is an acceptable play. If the ball touches my body, I'll lose the point. And at this distance—we're approximately ten feet apart—it would strike me with the force of a fist thrown by a man much larger than I.

Then something amazing happens. I somehow reflex my racket onto the ball, punching it right back at Tripp. The butt of his hand jams against his sternum as he tries to locate the ball with his racket, which he does, but just barely, and it flies over my head and far out of play. Tripp's eyebrows raise and he grins a sheepish smirk. It's a look of pure surprise.

I pump my fist and scream. This isn't irony. I'm not pretending. It's pure animal ecstasy, and it's something I haven't felt in a long time. Maybe not since the last time I played the drums.

"I thought for sure I was going to golden-set you," Tripp says later, referring to the term used when someone wins a set without allowing the other player to win a single point. "And I thought one million percent that, if I did not, it was going to be my fault. But to lose a point because you came up with a spectacular play at the net that I could not handle is not what I expected."

I could type that quote one million times.

That night, I wake up twice replaying the point in my mind. I'm just mining it for all that it's worth, using it to make myself feel like I'm some sort of secret tennis expert, one who only just now has begun to reveal himself, and the semi-delusional nature of this thought process reminds me of how I used to feel when I was younger and would play with a musician who was much better than I. Because invariably they would make me sound better than I could on my own, and afterward the thrill of hearing that new version of myself would linger with me, intoxicatingly, making me long for some way to make him appear again.

In the morning I watch a few Wimbledon highlights on ESPN and feel like, for the first time ever, I understand exactly what those players are feeling. Then a friend emails me a short video clip of the match, and when I see my actual form on the court I'm mortified. Just the way Tripp and I walk around the net between games reveals who's the athlete and who's the ex-drummer.

But still. On the first point of the second set I chip and charge again and put away another winner. For the span of a few seconds, as I stand there in triumph, I am ahead: 15–love, Brown.

It doesn't last. Of course it doesn't. I lose I lose I lose. But like all those musicians who once brought out the best in me, Tripp has coaxed a surprise version of myself onto the court on this day—he's that red-faced bald man screaming like an idiot there at net with his fist in the air—and that's the guy who's the winner. He's the one who's been waiting for so long to come out and play.

13 | THE WORDS

There's an uncomfortable conversation I have from time to time. It comes up when people who know me as a writer learn that I used to play drums in a band. "Oh, you must have written lyrics too," they say. No, I explain, I just played the drums. If pressed, I might add that the singer was always the one who came up with the lyrics, or that I sing so poorly I could never imagine trying to help, all of which is true. What I don't say, though, is that usually I can't even hear a song's lyrics, at least not in the way most people do. I can tell that words are being sung, yes, and the melody is entirely clear, but the words themselves? They scramble and float away from me, like I'm reaching out to grab a reflection on the surface of water.

If this seems strange, which I suppose it should, I never spent much time worrying about it. The voice wasn't my instrument. The drums were. End of story. As a kid obsessively listening to the Beatles and Led Zeppelin growing up, I just assumed all lyrics were nonsense. "Savoy Truffle." "Whole Lotta Love."

Choice phrases but little more. To me, lyrics were delivery devices for melody, and it was best not to waste too much time on the packaging.

Around the time my daughter turned eight, though, she started reciting the lyrics to pop songs with such ease and precision that it made me rethink my own relationship with them.

"These expensive, these is red bottoms," she sang from the backseat one afternoon. "These is bloody shoes."

"Wait, what?" I said.

She nodded toward the air, as if to point out that Cardi B was singing those exact words on the car stereo at that very moment.

"Well yeah," I said, "but how did you learn them?"

She shrugged, as if to ask, Why shouldn't I? The words were right there in the car with us.

She had a point. I tried to focus on the next verse myself, to see if I could absorb it all too, but the words were unreadable, and for the first time I started to wonder if something wasn't actually wrong with me. This pattern—of my daughter picking up lyrics with ease, and me failing to do so the same—went on for years until finally, one day at my computer, I typed "why can't I hear any lyrics?" into the search engine.

"It's even difficult for me to sit and to tell myself to pay attention to the singer, because I would feel too overwhelmed to continue," read one personal essay that I found called "What It's Like To Be Lyric Deaf," written by a college student named Annette Kim and posted on the website *Odyssey* in 2016. "I can't understand the context of spoken words within the song because I understand music differently. To me, songs have two distinct systems to be analyzed: the first system which I've

naturally preferred is the content and emotions within instru-
mentals, and the second system being voices. I hear singing
voices as another instrument, which is why I believe it has always been indistinguishable."

My god, I thought. I'm not alone.

I found more, too, at one point even attempting to read
a scientific study about how the brain processes melody differently from lyrics. And while much of what I read was of
interest, largely what I found didn't apply to me, because while
there were many people in the world who claimed to have this
so-called condition, what I didn't find were any who were "lyrically deaf" and also a musician, let alone a writer as well, and
that was the intersection I was most interested in. For me it
seemed like the two art forms I had spent my life pursuing had
created not an overlap of meaningful connection, but rather one
of erasure.

So I decided to force them together.

"Hey, what song should I learn the lyrics to?" I said, opening the door to my daughter's bedroom one day.

"Beastie Boys," she said. "Or wait—one of your songs. An
Athenaeum song."

My own band, Athenaeum. The one I played with all
through the nineties. Of all lyrics, you'd think I'd know ours. I
didn't, though, so I put on my headphones and started to listen.

Up first was "What I Didn't Know," our one radio hit. The
song opens with a four bar drum intro, and before the first measure was over, I found myself thinking about the high-pitched
ping ringing off each quarter note of the snare drum, wondering if I should have tuned it out or not, eventually coming to
the conclusion that it was probably better that I left it in, because

the drum sounded natural that way and a little unusual, but then when the rest of the band came in I started thinking about the way in which the sound of the snare changed when situated within the sonic context of two guitars and a bass—the ping seemingly gone now, even though we know it's still there—and now that the whole band was playing together, I was struck by how tight the eighth-note syncopation of the bass guitar and bass drum felt, a unit that surely would have been fashioned through some grid on Pro Tools today but was something we did organically back in 1997, and thus before I knew it, the verse was over and I had yet to listen to a single lyric.

This went on and on. No matter how hard I focused on what our singer was saying, I just kept getting distracted by the instrumentation. It was like I was a racehorse who couldn't run without blinders. Slowly, though, I managed to parse out each word, a laborious process that ended up being more like translation than memorization, because in a way the lyrics were all already there in my mind. I knew the rhythm of each one, how it was delivered, where the accents were, even where the breaths were taken. All I was doing now was decoding what the sound of each one meant.

I sang the song in the office. I sang it in the kitchen. And I sang while walking our dog, stopping at one point to laugh at myself as I struggled to remember the words to my own radio hit from twenty years before. This was a song I'd helped to write in my own attic, though, and I'd played it one million times. So of course I'd be able to learn the words eventually. It was time for something more challenging. Something more lyrically dense. Something, as my daughter had suggested, by the Beastie Boys.

Is it weird to love a rap band when you can't hear the lyrics? Maybe. But ever since I heard my brother's cassette of *Licensed to Ill* in 1986, the Beastie Boys have occupied a sweet spot in my mind. I chose as my assignment "So What'cha Want" off their 1992 album *Check Your Head*, because its tempo is 85 beats per minute, and that's the exact pace I like to run to, so often I put it on my headphones and match each step to an eighth note, as if my feet are my drumsticks and I'm playing along.

As soon as I started listening to the lyrics, though—pausing and rewinding and playing it back, refusing to cheat by looking anything up—I asked myself why I was bothering. I mean, lines like "Well just plug me in just like I was Eddie Harris / You're eating crazy cheese like you would think I'm from Paris" are funny, sure, but they didn't do much to shake my youthful conviction that lyrics were more than empty containers. Nevertheless, I persevered, and after learning the first verse, I waited until Abby and Frances left the house before I started to rap.

The first thing I noticed was how much breath it takes. And also my hands kept doing this karate chop thing, a tic I found mortifying, but couldn't seem to stop. Increasingly I became afraid that the UPS man would come to the door and see me or hear me, and finally, in fear of ruining the song entirely, I just quit and stood there panting.

There's a gap in my investigation here. Perhaps you've already noticed. The Beastie Boys and Cardi B and my old band from high school are not a representative selection of lyrical achievement. I know. So maybe you can tell I'm being selective with my choices. Misleading, even. And so you might ask,

What about the greats? What about the songwriters who are *known* for their lyrics?

Yeah. I can hear them. I think Bruce Springsteen's *Nebraska* was the first one that popped for me, like a switch had been flipped. The lyrics suddenly rising to the surface. That title track, the monologue from a convicted killer about a crime spree with his girlfriend. The detail of the girl spinning her baton when they first met. Then "Highway Patrolman," about a cop and his criminal brother. The scene where they both take turns dancing with the same girl, Maria. The specificity. The compression of language. How'd this guy learn to write like this? I thought. Where'd he get his MFA?

I can't stand Bruce Springsteen, though. At least not all that eighties stuff. All those blown-out production numbers with the horns and glockenspiels and that big big macho strut. I hated that shit. But this album. It was nothing. Just guitar and a voice. I loved it.

Perhaps the minimal production is what allowed me to notice the lyrics, but I think it was something more. I think I could hear them because the writing is great, and because I listened to the album at the right time to notice. This was during a period when I was living in New York and just starting to imagine myself as a writer. Suddenly I was on the lookout for sharp detail, evocation of place, three-dimensional characters, conflict, and scene building. And all these I found on *Nebraska*. But none of those are qualities I necessarily look for in music. They are what I read for. From music I expect something more, something visceral, like a chemical reaction. Because reading great writing is great, but when I hear the right combination of rhythm and melody—regardless of lyrics, or even without lyrics at all—what it does is elicit an animal desire in me. It's almost sexual in its nature. It makes me want to *play*.

I guess once you start thinking about your relationship to music as something you want to have sex with, though, it's time to seek help. So I requested an interview with a music psychologist who I found online—a man who held an important position at my university, and whose photo made me think of a stern Scandinavian judge. Most enticing, though, was the fact that this man's specialty was the study of Sun Ra, the avant-garde jazz musician who claimed to be an alien. Oh yes, I thought, if anyone is going to be game for some strange questions about lyric deafness, this is the guy. I wrote him a long email delving into many thoughts about music and lyrics, and then the man never responded.

I looked back at what I wrote. With a week or two of perspective, it did sound a bit crazy. I drafted a new and less rambling request to a different music psychologist, but then before I sent it, I found myself losing conviction. Was something actually wrong with me? I mean, I could hear some lyrics, couldn't I?

Around this time, I spent an evening in my living room with my daughter listening to the soundtrack from *Hamilton*. She, of course, knew every word, and I, of course, knew none of them. I didn't waste time trying to learn them, though, because I was too busy playing along with my hands and my feet. I'd mess with words in the morning. That's when I'd sit at my desk and inspect different ones like gemstones, hefting, searching for just the right hue. For now, I was happy to be working with different materials. And it occurred to me that maybe that's my problem. Maybe I'm just so in love with music that it's one of those things that can make you a little bit blind. Because when I try to shake it off and focus on something else, I just can't. Why would I, though? It's hard to not love love. So even though I've spent years telling everyone I'm a writer and no longer a drummer, I'm starting to think you shouldn't believe it. Because those are just words. Don't even listen to them.

Nathan had a rehearsal space in one of those storage units where the lights run on a windup timer. Sometimes, in the middle of a song, the timer would run out, but we wouldn't stop. We'd just play on in the dark.

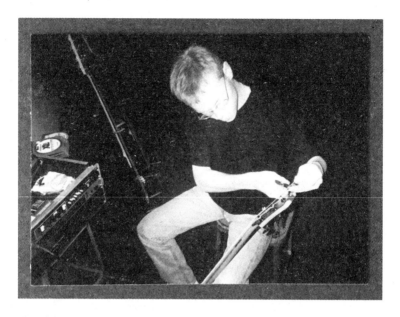

Alex liked to call each town by the wrong nickname. "Ah, the Windy City," he said as we rolled into Atlanta. "The City of Brotherly Love," he said, coming out of the Lincoln Tunnel into Midtown Manhattan. "The Twin Cities, wow," he said as the Gateway Arch appeared over the Eads Bridge in St. Louis. I'm not sure anyone else ever noticed, but I always thought it was hilarious.

I pressed my forehead against the windowpane in my room one night, around two or three. This was on the third floor of a hotel that seemed to have been built on the edge of a great field. The only light came from the swimming pool below, an oval of turquoise glowing against a vast sea of black. I looked down and found Christian there, standing alone in the shallow end, smoking a cigarette. It looked like he was waiting for something.

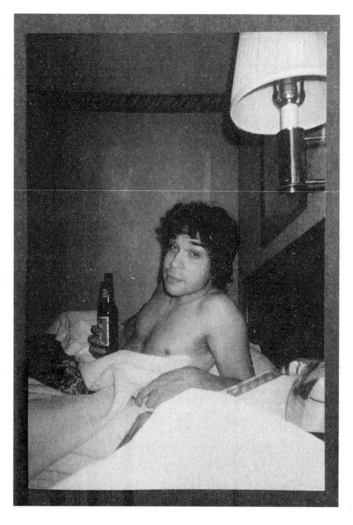

Dave asked if this picture was taken in the morning or at night.

John was the most famous producer we'd worked with by far, so Shannon and I wanted to know what he thought. We sat quietly in the shadows, hanging on every word, while a computer displayed the tracks as a sequence of colorful shapes, overlapping and intertwined on the monitor before him. John's head was bent over. He listened closely. "Look," he finally said, looking up at the screen. "That looks like a Navajo blanket."

Joey handed me a photograph of Thelonious Monk as I entered the school auditorium, where we were taking the SAT. "This is for luck," he said, and folded it into my pocket. He was obsessed with Monk. After taking my seat, the exam proctor approached. It was my biology teacher. "I saw you with that sheet of paper," he said, looking into my pocket. "It's just a picture of Thelonious Monk," I said, handing him the photograph. The man considered it for a moment, as if to decode how it could be used to cheat. "Joey gave it to me," I said. Then the man nodded, like everything made sense now, and returned it.

Jeff's father was a professor of piano performance, but the keyboard parts Jeff played with us were just simple bass lines, often requiring no more than one finger.

Chris told Abby one morning that he liked his coffee with enough milk in it to turn it the color of a brown paper bag. For years I thought of that every time I added milk to my own coffee. Then when I started drinking it black a few years later, I felt bad, like I was letting a piece of him go.

Erik made puppets.

Steve told me a story about his father once, about how he dug a ditch in the backyard and started spending time in it. He even brought some furniture out and put it in there. "He called it MUD," Steve said. "My Underground Development." I think about that story a lot.

15 | THE ACCOMPANIST

I see a woman at a piano during an audition. A woman at a piano during a choral performance. A woman at a piano supporting a company of ballet dancers. It's always a woman, it seems, always at a piano, always unsmiling, busy, and focused. You've seen her before. She's that most unheralded of musical professionals—the accompanist—and in a lifetime of playing the drums, I'm sure I've performed with one once. If I have, though, I have forgotten, but this seems only right; accompanists are meant to go unnoticed. They mete out their chords humbly from the side of the stage, the spotlight shining instead upon the true star of the show—that unsure student or wobbly dancer or brash, flashy soloist.

Never have I questioned why accompanists do what they do. Never asked what is in it for them. It is not until I am the one preparing to do some accompanying myself that any of this comes to mind, because now that I'm here, I'm wondering, *Why the hell am I here?*

It's 6:00 p.m., an hour before showtime, and I'm wearing a dark navy suit and a white shirt and am standing on the stage of the Oconee Hall at Tri-County Technical College in Pendleton, South Carolina. Beside me is Jeff Christmas, the Tri-County Jazz Band director, and together we're looking into what I had thought was the dressing room, but which appears to be nothing more than an oversized storage closet filled with hundreds of boxes of Weight Watchers cookies.

"It's because the local chapter meets here on weekends," Jeff says.

"Local Weight Watchers chapter?" I say.

"Yeah," he says, and we laugh. Not because of Weight Watchers, but because Jeff knows tonight is going to be my first performance in something like eight years, and that wherever it was I played last, it surely didn't have a backstage filled up with cookies. We don't have time to dwell on any of that, though. Right now we need to run through "All Blues" with the students again, so I toss my cases in with the cookies and take my place at the drums.

Two saxophone players, one trumpet player, an acoustic guitarist, and Jose. This is the lineup. Jose doesn't play an instrument, though, so Jeff has him on bass. It isn't a proper band, obviously—this is the first semester the class has been offered, so enrollment was low—but that's why I'm here. Jeff has had to call in the pros: a young piano player whose day job is selling menswear at Belk, and me.

I'd thought I was going to be like some retired big leaguer coming back to coach Little League. That this would be my chance to give back. To reap some karmic reward. I've been coming to rehearsals for weeks, though, and it's been unbearable.

The students aren't yet good at their instruments. The tempos are all over the place. The dynamics are a mess. And though my own chops have remained pretty sharp, it's hard to play well with people who can't play. It feels like trying to dance in a rowboat in waves. All of which could be predictable, and completely acceptable, I guess, if not for the fact that on top of it all, no one seems to be having much fun. Fear of mistakes is the dominant vibe. And it's not like anyone's very thankful for my appearance here either. Jeff is, of course—he's a good friend, which is the reason I've come—but the students all just give me the silent treatment and the side eye, as if I'm someone of whom they should be suspicious. And maybe they should be. Maybe they know that I'm dreading every moment I spend playing with them. Maybe they know that for me, tonight's show has arrived like a reward, simply because it's the end.

At seven, lights dim. Family and friends grow quiet in their seats. A baby cries out in the darkness. Abby and Frances are here too, and even though Frances is eight, it's going to be the first time she will have seen me perform on a stage. I resent that this is the place where it's going to happen.

The set is three songs. Our first, "All Blues," sounds bad. The next one, "Take the A Train," sounds bad too. And then during the final song—a showtune sung by a young woman holding the microphone so far from her mouth that no one can hear her—one of my hands slips during a drum fill and I flub a note. Jeff looks at me knowingly. It feels like a bruise on my heart.

At last, the show's over, but before the final note can even fade away, a group of young women in white appears in the wings. This is the chorus, due to perform next, and at once they start pushing a three-tier bleacher-like structure onto the stage. Half-panicked because of their haste, Jose unplugs his bass without turning off the amp and a loud pop booms through the room. The horn players dash off with music stands rattling against hips. Breaking down drums can take forever, though, so I opt to shove them into the Weight Watchers closet for now.

One by one I shuttle them in, but just as I'm setting down the last drum, my world goes suddenly black. I spin in confusion. Someone, it seems, has shut the door behind me. I knock over a few boxes of cookies trying to make my way back to it, but before I can get there, the chorus breaks into song. It's something from *West Side Story*, and as the first muffled notes swell through the walls, I realize I'm stuck. The door opens onto the stage. Even if I were to get there now, my only option would be to emerge into the middle of the performance.

I start laughing. It's just too much: my first show back, and I end up locked in a storage closet filled with cookies.

Slowly, as my eyes adjust to the dark, the cookies come into focus. Oat and Caramel Chip Breakfast Cookies. Oat and Chocolate Chip Breakfast Cookies. Oat and Mixed Berry Breakfast Cookies. I've never heard of a breakfast cookie before. I'm not sure cookies for breakfast is the best message for someone trying to improve their diet, but what do I know. I figure if I'm going to be stuck in here with them, though, I might as well eat one, but then when I reach out to grab a package, its plastic coating crinkles so loudly that I freeze, scared I'll be heard by the audience, and I remain like that, immobile, gripping a package of Weight Watchers cookies in fear in the dark.

All the driving to and from campus. All the hauling of cases up and down stairs and the hours of bumpy rehearsal. All that and now this. I understand there's something deeply funny about the whole situation, but at the same time I'm a little pissed off. I promise myself I will never put myself in a position like this again. Never.

A few days later I'm surprised to hear Abby on the phone telling her friend about how beautiful the performance was. That the fact that the show was not good was the best part about it. That it was inspiring.

Abby is deaf in one ear and most of the way in the other. She was born that way. She reads lips and gets along fine, but music is a different experience for her than it is for me. As far as I know, singing "Happy Birthday" is about the extent of her experience as a musical performer, so I'm blindsided when, a week or two later, she asks to borrow one of her father's guitars and starts watching clips on YouTube about how to play "I Won't Back Down" by Tom Petty. She says that not everything has to be perfect to be meaningful. That the Tri-County show has taught her this. That it made playing music seem possible.

Over the next few weeks, the chords to "I Won't Back Down" waft down the stairs, slow and unsure and deliberate. I freeze when I hear them, afraid that Abby might catch me and stop. I wonder if this is what "All Blues" sounded like to Jose's family that night at Tri-County Tech. If this is what the mothers and fathers of the chorus members felt as their children sang while I clutched my cookies in fear in the dark. Because even though Abby isn't playing Tom Petty's song perfectly, I listen to her in astonishment—it's like an announcement from the woman I thought I knew every part of, telling me there is so much yet to discover.

The next time Jeff asks me to help him out, it's to accompany a group of children giving a piano recital at the Unitarian church. This is a yearly event. The children—all students of a local piano teacher named Donna—each select a favorite pop song to learn, and then Donna pulls together a band to perform with them. "I'm With the Band!" is what she calls it. Jeff is the singer.

At first I think no. There's no way I'm getting involved in something like this again. But my daughter has begun taking lessons with Donna. And the show is all for the kids. I try to maintain my resistance, but at last I relent.

On the day of the performance, the air conditioning breaks in the church. It's June in South Carolina. Which is to say it is humid and hot. I sweat through my white oxford shirt while Donna keeps asking if I can play quieter, even though I'm play-ing as quietly as it is possible to play on a drum set. The other musicians are a motley assortment of locals, including the as-sociate provost of the university where I teach, who is wearing a Yes T-shirt and playing bass through a large neon green rig, as well as a young high school student who blasts out a solo on his tenor saxophone so loud and incongruous to the whole setting that I can only look at Jeff in shock. No one seems to have learned their parts very well, and I am both embarrassed at the amount of time I spent on the songs—several afternoons, during which I wrote out a chart for each number—while also frustrated that I didn't spend even more time on them. Because maybe then I could have made us sound better. And we do not sound very good.

At least my daughter's song goes well. Wisely she chose a number that didn't require the full band at all—hers is just piano with Jeff singing—and so when they begin, the whole room seems to sigh in relief. Soon the band gears up again, though, and again we sound terrible, and again Donna asks me to play more quietly, and again I promise myself I will never do this again.

The next year I do it again.

My daughter has chosen a song to play with the whole band this time. I can't let someone else be her drummer. So of course I say yes.

At least this year the AC is working, but other than that, not much has changed. Again the sax player rips an outrageously loud solo. Again Donna asks me to play more quietly than is possible. And again no one seems to have learned their parts very well. If anything, though, the show feels more comfortable than before, if only because I know what to expect.

Then we play "Tiny Dancer."

The boy who picked this song—the Elton John classic—can only make it through a few chords before stopping and restarting and skipping ahead and then back. It sounds as if he might never have practiced it once. And while a bass or guitar can let a note hang, the drums have nowhere to hide. Every lurch and stop and start is like a train rumbling off its tracks. Playing that song that afternoon is easily the worst I have ever felt during any performance of any music ever, and the selfish mortification of the whole episode remains so potent with me that by the time my daughter gets up to play with us, I hardly even notice it's happening. Her song is excellent, if only because she had the luxury/torture of practicing at home with me so many times, but instead of enjoying that rare opportunity to share a stage with my daughter, I just keep thinking about "Tiny Dancer," my mind spinning around all that went wrong, until the next thing I know, my daughter is done.

I realize now, though, that I might never have a chance to perform like that with her again. She's quit taking music lessons since that day. Like so many parental realizations that come to me after the fact, I wish I'd appreciated the moment more as it was happening.

The funny thing is, when my daughter cranks up "Tiny Dancer" on the radio these days—something she still likes to do just to watch me recoil in pain—what I think of most is not the disastrous performance of that song on that day, but rather how I accompanied my daughter right afterward, and how easy that was, and how well she performed, and how we did it together. She's almost thirteen now, which means three years have already passed since that show. In another three, she'll be driving, and then three more after that she'll be gone. So even though I still cringe when I hear "Tiny Dancer," I'm growing to love it as well. It's a reminder of not just one special moment in my life, but how I can't let any more of them slip past.

Donna's concert was canceled this past year because of the pandemic, news that came as a welcome relief, despite the begrudging appreciation I've developed for those shows over time. And though Frances continues to turn up the volume when "Tiny Dancer" comes on, and Abby still strums the chords to "I Won't Back Down," I was surprised recently to discover the ways in which my work as an accompanist stretched beyond the walls of our home.

It was during a vigil for George Floyd this past summer, when a hundred or so of us knelt on the lawn at the center of our city. The pandemic was raging, as was the reign of Donald Trump, and in this small southern town where I live—one where an armada of pickup trucks flying Confederate flags had just driven past, slowly and pointedly—I had begun to feel not only disconnected with my community, but even angry at the people within it. People I knew, people who I loved even, many of whom were supporters of Trump and had been telling me and my family things like Covid was "going to end the day after the election," and that they were "not racist, *but . . .*" they were "getting tired of this Black Lives Matter stuff." So it was powerful to be on that lawn that day with my wife and daughter, among like-minded people. Still, I couldn't even tell who we were with. Everyone was masked, we were all socially distanced, and for almost nine minutes we had been kneeling in silence.

Then a young man stood up with a saxophone. Pulling notes from the air with great difficulty, he performed "Amazing Grace" in a wobbly and uncertain performance. And yet it could not have been more moving. People began to tear up—I began to tear up—and then in shock I realized I knew the man. It was that young saxophone player from Donna's band, the one who had ripped all those wild solos in church. I waved at him, strangely thrilled to have any connection to the man currently bringing so many people to tears, but he didn't see me. Or if he did, he looked right through me. I was just an invisible face to him, an accompanist lost in a sea of accompanists that day, because what were we all doing there together if not supporting one another's unsure performances on a stage that had somehow become unfamiliar and treacherous? Just knowing I'd been his drummer, though, made me feel a connection to my community as potent as any I've felt in my life. It was right when I'd been feeling most isolated in the world that he stood up and played, reminding me with just a few notes that I wasn't alone there at all. In fact, I was part of a band.

16 | HOW TO PLAY A REUNION SHOW WITH YOUR BAND FROM THE NINETIES

First you think about it.

This part can go on for years.

And then one night, while your wife is doing bedtime with your daughter upstairs, a few former Carolina basketball players pop up on the television, talking about the team. About the days when they were on it. About how they will always treasure that family. About how much they love coach. You're moved by these basketball players, who somehow make you miss your own days on the team, even though of course you were never on any basketball team, let alone the Carolina one. But you were once in a successful band, and when you think about that band sometimes you feel the way these now-crying basketball players seem to feel about their team. Which is to say you can miss it.

You know that if you keep thinking about it, though, you'll find yet another reason not to text that band's singer, Mark, about playing a reunion show—because, really, is there anything more embarrassing than getting your old nineties band back together for one last hurrah? You do not allow the question to linger. Instead, you pick up your phone.

Hey! you type. *20th anniversary of the Radiance release coming up on April 8 . . . Should we do something? Like a show? Is that crazy? That's crazy, right?* Something with a built-in eject button.

But Mark doesn't eject. He just calmly replies with *yeah, that could be cool. I'll talk to Alex.*

Days pass.

The longer you're away from the tearful basketball players on your television screen, the more any reunion of your band seems like an exercise in dredging up the most embarrassing parts of your past. Like that time you wore a black satin sparkly shirt to the Blind Tiger. Or when you used to cup your hand to your ear as if the crowd wasn't cheering loudly enough. Or when you fired your first manager. Or your second. Or when you were sued for it. More than any of that, though, it's the music itself you're bashful about. Because although it once filled you with pleasure, that was in high school, and in the years since, your tastes have changed, which was one reason you quit in the first place. So is it a good idea to go back now? You're not sure.

When it becomes clear that Grey won't be playing the show—
Grey is the original guitarist—you see your chance to back out.

I'm just not sure if it'll be right without the original lineup, you say.
OK, Mark says. *Just think about it.*

Return to step one.

In the meantime, you go on a magazine assignment—you're
a writer now, not a drummer—during which you stand in a
field with a famous ornithologist and giggle about the fact that
a bird is named a dickcissel. You take notes on the dickscissel
birdsong, on what the ornithologist does with his Nikon, on
how the wind moves through the grasses. These are the details
that bring a piece to life. It's reporting 101. Or you guess it is.
You've never really taken a journalism class. But something
about putting yourself into the field with this man provides
all the material you need for your article, a truth that has been
borne out so many times over so many assignments that you
now understand it to be a pillar upon which you can rely.
You have recently been thinking about writing something
longer than an article, though, something about your past as
a drummer, because your new novel is feeling sort of dead
right now and it seems weird to have this phantom drummer
identity living within you, especially when you never drum
anymore or even really talk about it, and so maybe that could
be an interesting thing to write about instead. But if you do
end up writing about your past as a drummer, you know
you'll have to do some reporting. Just like for this article on

the ornithologist, you'll need to go live on the scene. And a reunion would be the ultimate scene.

OK, you write back to Mark. *Let's do this thing.*

In the press release, they spell the band's name wrong. On Instagram, they spell the band's name wrong. In the email that your old high school sends to all alumni about the show, a transmission that makes you cringe at the thought of all the former crushes deleting it from their inboxes, they at least spell the name right. The *Winston-Salem Journal* runs an article, in which you are quoted as saying that playing a rock show as a forty-year-old is "innately embarrassing." Online, Linda from Ohio says *OH MY GAWD I KNOW EVERY WORD TO RADIANCE I STILL PLAY IT FOR MYSELF AND ENLIGHTEN OTHERS* 😊 *THIS POST MADE MY DAY/LIFE AND SEEING IT WAS DESTINY THANK YOU THANK YOU* 😳 ✖️✖️ 😇 😜 😀 Burt from Michigan says *FAVORITE BAND OF ALL TIME. NEVER HAD A CHANCE TO SEE, NOW I DO!!! ROAD TRIP FROM DETROIT!!!!* Kimmy from Chattanooga says *OH!!! YES!!!! GOING!!!! MET MY HUSBAND BECAUSE OF THIS BAND!!!!!!* 💜💜💜💜

It is strange to see these reactions from strangers. But then again, maybe they aren't strangers. This is 2018—just click on their face. One is a nurse. Another works at Wendy's. Someone else sells industrial lighting. No, you don't know these people. It feels like you've reopened a room that all along you'd thought was just yours, only to discover that all these other people had been living in there the whole time.

Seventy-one tickets sell the first day.

One hundred fifty-three tickets sell over the next two days.

Is this a lot? It doesn't feel like it. The theater holds one thousand people.

You retrieve your drums from the basement and carry them into your guest room, where you set up away from all windows. Your neighbors know you only as an English professor who likes to work in the yard. The thought of them seeing or hearing you play drums is preemptively mortifying. In fact, you become so embarrassed at this prospect that you call the university music department, asking if they might have a practice room for you to use there instead, but after being told that the only options available are spaces shared with students, you decide to use the guest room after all, where you end up playing so lightly during that first day that you develop a strange cramp on the front of your shin from attempting to play the bass drum without making any sound. Eventually you settle on a low-volume tap, which you execute for a few weeks while listening to your old band's albums on headphones, the way you used to when you were a child and would play along with the Beatles. Except now you're playing along with yourself.

Bryce says he's driving up for the show. Your high school girlfriend too—she's coming down from D.C. People have booked trips from out of the country. Still, only two hundred and "seventyish" tickets have sold after thirteen days, according to the email you receive from Mark. You worry the room will be empty.

The first rehearsal takes place in a dingy studio behind the Greensboro Coliseum, a space packed with the gear of musicians whose names you remember. That's Eddie's cymbal stand. Jason's PA, yeah, it's fine. Andy won't mind if you use the Ampeg. It's all comforting, in a way, to know those guys are still around, and it's nice to be with your friends again too, band members you have not seen in years, men who used to live with you and record with you and whose dreams came true with you and whose farts you have smelled one million times. There's barely a need to even speak with them now. Not that you don't want to—you could talk for hours, catching up on families and work—but you've come together for something more mysterious and intimate: You've come to make music. And though it's been twenty years, you feel certain all will sound fine. All does not sound fine, though. What all sounds like is a bunch of scrap metal thrown into a turbine.

The show is three weeks away. You wait until your wife and daughter have both left the house before you stand in your downstairs bathroom, in front of the full-length mirror, with an armful of clothes. You have gone bald since you last played with this band, but you don't want anyone to think you're trying to cover it up. So, no hat. Also you will wear your

L.L.Bean Blucher moccasins, shoes your friend Matthew described as "the footwear of a middle school principal," as proof that you're not afraid to wear shoes that are uncool. And you'll keep your round tortoiseshell glasses on too, just to double down on the fact that you're forty and not twenty and you know it. But then you wonder if you have made so much of an effort not to look cool that you actually won't look cool. So you try on some T-shirts. You look like a forty-year-old bald guy in a T-shirt. You are also thinner than you were back when you used to play in this band. Recently a student described you as looking like Voldemort. You decide a blue button-down will have to suffice.

The second rehearsal is an improvement. You don't even understand what you're doing differently, but the songs sound like actual songs now. In fact, they sound good. You take out your earplugs. It's shocking after all this time to hear the sound of your instruments at full volume. You know at once that your ears will ring for days afterward. Still, you keep them out. You play even harder.

Your mother, your daughter, your wife, and your high school girlfriend all drive to the show in one car. Bryce and Liz come early so they can see you beforehand, as does Bryce's older brother, your former manager, the woman who used to tend bar at the Blind Tiger, your old neighbor Will, Joey's brother John, a classmate of your older brother's whose name you cannot recall but you think is something like Blythe, Scott

Carle, a current colleague from Clemson who turns out to have been a longtime fan and even wears an Athenaeum crop top that she bought in 1998 and has kept all these years, and so on and so on until it becomes clear that this reunion is not a reunion of band members so much as it is a reunion of all the people who bought the band's T-shirts and lived with its members in rental houses and took Intro to Spanish with them and made out with them in parked cars on weeknights by Buffalo Creek.

You and Mark peek through the curtains. Already a crowd is pressed against the front of the stage, a crowd that fills the whole room. A thousand people or more. It's a sellout, finally, and while you're looking at all those faces, including so many you recognize, the promoter surprises you by asking what no one else has.

"So, why'd you guys decide to finally do this?" he says.

Mark pulls his head from the curtains.

"Yeah, Nic, why did you decide to do this?" he says. Then, to the promoter, "It was Nic's idea."

You don't tell them that you're just a writer here on assignment. You know that's not the real reason. Or not the whole one, at least. The other part is the crying basketball players part, but you fear any attempt to explain that. So instead you just shrug and say, "I don't know."

But you feel like Mark knows. Because he too spent his youth making music with you in your attic, dreaming of getting a record deal, and now twenty years have gone by since that dream came true and you both know you'll never have another childhood to fill up with dreams again. So your performance tonight will be like one giant séance, bringing those dreams back to life, a ceremony that can only work if you are all gathered in one place together. But it can't just be you and Mark and Alex and Mike, you now understand. It has to be with Linda from Ohio too, and Burt from Michigan, and Bryce and Scott Carle and your mother and your daughter. Only with all of them here in one room can you imagine feeling the way you feel now, which is grateful and loved and surprised. And so you guess that's why you're here.

The walkie-talkie on John's shoulder crackles.

Five minutes, he says.

Several guitar cases are propped open around you, their plush velvet insides exposed, and for a moment you wish you could climb into one of them and have it close over you.

Two minutes, John says. Then OK, let's go to the stairs.

The stage is like a private balcony from which you can watch the crowd in peace. No more surprise interaction. Everything up there is relaxed and rehearsed, as easy as walking a line. Beyond is the turmoil. Past the edge of the stage is where a crush of people—so many who you recognize, even if you don't know their names—are now singing and dancing, although several also seem to be crying. And for what? Not the music, you think, even though you are indeed performing these songs better than you ever have. Each band member has, in the past twenty years, improved greatly as a musician. But no, those tears are not for your songs. They are surely for the sudden awareness of all that has happened to everyone since those songs were first heard. Because while you're up there playing the same notes as you did at nineteen, you are now bald. And you have a nine-year-old daughter watching from the side of the stage, and a wife too. And surely these crying people now have wives and daughters and bald heads too, ones that didn't exist when they first heard these songs, and if you feel like you're experiencing some type of double existence—like it is both you and the ghost of yourself up there hitting the crash—then maybe these people have become aware of their own ghosts in the room, dancing along with them too, and maybe they are surprised by that appearance, shocked to find that they have already lived enough life to yet have a ghost.

After the show you try to be patient. But your wife and daughter and mother have already left and it's long after your bedtime and you want to talk to Bryce and to Scott Carle and to Eddie Walker before they leave too and so finally you just do it, you step out of the green room and walk around the side of the stage, where you're met by a swell of people pressing the barricade, many holding old posters and CDs and shirts. "Oh my god, look at his shoes," you hear one woman say, which you think is funny, but then this woman turns out to be very drunk and asks for a photo with you and then another photo with you and then hey, come over here, let's take one with Henry and wait do you remember and you start to think maybe coming out here wasn't such a good idea after all when finally someone pulls you away. You thank him and he introduces himself. He is a handsome blond man. He used to come hear you when he was younger, he says, back when blah blah would sneak him in because he was too young to get into the shows and he was a teenager then and so on and so on and again you start to think that maybe you shouldn't have left the backstage after all but then this man says, "And I don't know if you remember but when you were a teenager and Atlantic Records made you a fake ID . . ."

How could this man know this story, about when you were nineteen and an A&R rep got frustrated because you couldn't get into clubs and so demanded someone get you a fake ID, a task your road manager did indeed accomplish within days? You haven't thought of it in forever.

Well, the man goes on to explain, he was the one who came to a show back in some year and couldn't get in because he was underage and you ran into him in the lot and you had just turned twenty-one and so you gave him that fake ID and told him to keep it. Do you remember?

The dual existence happens again, like a switch has been flipped, and suddenly you are both looking at this man in the theater right now while also looking at his teenage face in a parking lot in 1998. And you recognize him. You can see him, not as he is but as he was. He's young and blond and standing in late afternoon sunlight behind a theater and he's excited about the show and even more excited about the ID you're giving to him, but then when he runs off with it you suddenly become convinced that he will get arrested and it will all come back to haunt you and so you start to look for him frantically but you can't find him, and in fact, you never see him again. Not until now. Not until this man, now twenty years older, is telling you that he did indeed keep that ID all these years, that he even brought it with him tonight, and that a friend—a man in a blue hat behind him—came with him too, and that the Blue Hat Man left his wallet behind and so actually used that fake ID to get in tonight and can you believe it? No, you say, you can't.

Because how can that be true? But the Blue Hat Man pulls your old fake ID from his shirt pocket and hands it to you and as you marvel at the return of this strange object—one that features an unsmiling photo of you at the age of nineteen, wearing a green Sanitary Fish Restaurant T-shirt—the men position themselves on either side of you while someone flashes a photo.

A hand squeezes your shoulder—you're afraid it's that drunk from before, but it isn't, you're happy to see, just someone who wants to say hi—and when you turn back, the two men are gone. Your former identity is still in your hands, though, the one you thought had been lost forever. And at once it all becomes clear. This is what you have come for. This is the song of the dickcissel. The wind whipping grasses. Your ID is the prop around which a story might build.

You need to take some notes right away, you think, but you don't have a notepad and the prospect of typing into your phone in front of people has always left you feeling bashful, so you make your way to the loading dock where, when you step outside—leaving the doors cracked behind you so you won't get locked out—you are shocked to find snow in the air. Never before have you seen snow fall in April in North Carolina.

It's snowing in April, you type into your phone. *And some guy just gave me my old fake ID. The return of my old identity! It's too perfect. Time feels all messed up. My ears are ringing so hard it's exhausting. My head hurts a lot. But it might also be because I haven't eaten in hours? I took two ibuprofen . . .*

You keep typing, feeling as if you're touching the essence of things, like your ID is some magic totem granting access to all of your past. It is a feeling that will stretch forward in time, beyond that snowy loading dock and into the next several weeks, a period during which you will carry the fake ID in your wallet and show it to anyone willing to look. You will even slip a Toad the Wet Sprocket CD into the stereo of your '99 Volvo one afternoon—music that would have otherwise embarrassed you, because you feel it is uncool now and the soundtrack of your past—and you will be shocked to find the songs that meant so much to you in high school suddenly mean so much again. You will drive extra loops around campus, just to have more time to listen. There's the one you played with your eyes closed in the rain one night while parked at the curb outside Bryce's apartment by the School of the Arts. And the other one you liked to put on at sunset in your old bedroom in high school, sitting on the edge of the mattress, watching your pale curtains change color in the shifting light. Each note again sounds of that magic. You spin through six or seven CDs like this, all from your past, all restored to their power.

Alas, it will fade. You will once again stand in an orange classroom and try to convince your students to read Alice Munro; you will once again do bedtime with your daughter and run alone through the Clemson Experimental Forest and come home and sketch out notes for your new book, a project that will start to feel like it is coming together, but as it does you will lose that ability to listen to Toad the Wet Sprocket again. You will stop rewatching YouTube clips of the reunion show. You will no longer check to see if people have posted new memories on the Athenaeum Facebook page. And so when Mark writes to say that the Cat's Cradle has asked if you want to play New Year's Eve with Dillon Fence, you will feel like you're quitting the band all over again when you say that you don't want to do it. That you don't think you should play together again until there's another show that can be as special as the last one, a bit of logic that—if you follow the math—implies twenty more years must pass before you will perform again. At which point you will be sixty, an age that's surely unreachable, even though twenty feels like just a few weeks ago.

For now, though, you're still in the snow, tapping away at your phone—the portal in time has just opened—when someone shuffles behind you. You turn, in fear of being locked out, and find a security guard there. He's pulling the door shut.

"Wait!" you say.

The guard takes you in—you're just some guy wearing the shoes of a middle school principal.

"Who are you?" he says.

You don't tell him that you're a writer or a professor or a father or that you've spent the entire night—if not the last twenty years—trying to answer the very question he has just asked. Instead what you say is "I'm the drummer," and he nods, and pulls the door closed. But not all the way. Just enough to keep out the cold.

EPILOGUE | SOME QUESTIONS I HAVE ABOUT THE FUTURE

When Shannon tells me that he and Neil are planning to record some songs later on in the summer, and they're wondering if I want to join them, the first thing I ask is can I even go? Because how do we know the pandemic will be over by then? And how would I get to the studio? Fly? Drive?

None of which addresses the bigger question, though, which is do I even want to do this?

I've always said that Shannon and Neil were the only ones who could get me out of my musical exile, or whatever this is that I've been in for so long, so I guess I've known for a while—well before they ever asked—that I wanted to make new music with them again, but if I do so now, after all this time, what am I doing? Will I be opening a whole can of worms? Like, will people hear about me doing this and think I'm trying to be a working musician again?

Then again, what "people" am I worried might hear about this?

Is anyone left who might care?

How much is the RV Abby found on Facebook Marketplace? And is that even the one she's thinking of renting for us, or is that the one she wants to buy and put on the back end of the lot as a little studio? If we do take an RV to California, where will we stop on the way? Iowa and Colorado are both on the route, aren't they? Will Jamie be around? Or Dan?

The studio is what they call a residential studio, which means you stay on the premises, and in the photos online it seems to be huge, almost like a castle, and I see that My Morning Jacket did an album there, and Feist too, so that's all promising, but why are they being so vague about the accommodations? Shannon reminds me that this is a studio, not an Airbnb, and so the studio manager is not a hotel manager, a reminder that then reminds me of something else, which is that studio accommodations are invariably funky—if not simply bad, no matter how "nice" the studio—and so I begin to wonder, if I can't even tell my family where they'll be sleeping, is it really a good idea to make plans for them to drive across the country with me?

So do we want to fly instead?

Have you seen the rates?

Should I go alone?

Is my floor tom really this mildewy because I haven't played it in so long?

Hey Shannon, do you know what drums they have at the studio? And can you get a list of the cymbals for me? Or should I just ship my cymbals from here?

Can the neighbors hear me practicing? And if so, will they insist on talking to me about drumming? Will they say, "Hey Nic, when can we hear your band?" Or "Hey, you getting back into it?!"

How can I make sure to avoid this?

On the plane, do I tell the truth to the cybersecurity expert seated beside me when he asks why I'm flying to California? And since he's a security expert, can he tell that I'm lying?

When we arrive at the studio—which Shannon is proud of having "undersold," because it is much more impressive than I had imagined—I look out at the view of Bolinas Bay beyond the gravel parking space, and even though Shannon is looking at the very same water at the exact same moment as I am, and he's right beside me, I still say, "Man, you see that view?"

Does the engineer know that the clothes he's wearing—the slightly too-short dirtbag jeans, the no-brand sweatshirt, the filthy plain white sneakers—are pretty much the same thing everyone on the Lower East Side wore back when they came out to see us? And is that why he's wearing them? Like, did he google our band and see that Shannon once toured with the Strokes and then think, Oh, I need to dress like the Strokes?

"You tour around?" he says, as he's setting up mics, and then, "Oh, cool, where do you teach?"

Neil, are you good?

Do you have the click?

What channel are the vocals on?

Can you give me more bass?

What channel are the vocals on again?

Hey, is the click the right speed?

And hey, are you rolling?

Wait wait wait, where are the vocals again?

OK, Shannon says after the take, Nic, can you do more like a Ringo thing there? With the big fill? And then the chicka-chicka on the hats?

Yeah, I say, sure, wondering why didn't I think of that? How did Shannon just suggest a part that sounds more like my own style than the part I'd been playing? Or maybe my own style has always been his? Or is there any difference? Because isn't that what playing music is all about? Collaboration? And then I start to ask myself—would I be a better writer if I was collaborating with someone all the time, like I am here, instead of just working alone every day? And is that why I write instead of play drums now? Because it is easier? Like, am I in hiding? Or is it actually easier? Because isn't this song coming together pretty easily right now?

Hey Nic, you want to come hear this?

Hey Mandy, do you want to come hear this? Ellen?

You guys want dinner first?

No, listen, will you come down and listen to this? Isn't it great?

When the coyotes scream just outside my door after midnight, I fall back asleep pretty quickly, but then later I wake up again when I hear a different sound, and I sit up, thinking, *Is that the click?* It's not the coyotes—this is a steady, nonstop ticking that I hear—it sounds just like the click track, that electronic metronome that plays in our headphones to set tempo for us as we play, but I'm sleeping inside a small cabin—really a Tuff Shed—and it doesn't even have electricity, and it's on the side of a mountain, and unattached to the studio, so how could this be? And yet there it is, no doubt, a ticking and ticking, so am I just dreaming? Or have the guys gone out of their minds? Are they still in there recording? And if so, why are they playing a click track so loud that I can hear it out here on the side of a mountain? What time is it anyway? I check the time on my wristwatch, which is looped around the metal water bottle I tucked next to the pillow, and then I have a sudden thought: Could the ticking just be my wristwatch? Because it sounds like it's coming from something right beside me, and the water bottle is right beside me, and it has my watch on it, and the bottle itself could be working as some type of resonator, so I reach out and grab the bottle and sure enough the ticking stops right then, so yeah, it was just my wristwatch, but this leaves me with an even bigger question, which is why did I think it was a click track in the first place? Because how would that make any sense? Has something already changed so much inside me that I'm hearing the whole world like it's part of a recording session?

When we laugh and shake our heads and silently ask ourselves if we are geniuses, is this embarrassing? Or is it more embarrassing when we start to voice it aloud, saying *Hey, Neil, do you think we're actually geniuses?* Or *Hey, Shannon, when was the last time you were in a band that you were sure was the best band in the whole world?*

In the mornings, when the fog moves across the hillside in such thick threads of mist that it looks like smoke, should I take a photo? And then when I do, should I erase all the photos on my phone, because I see now that none of them capture even one small bit of what I feel is so special about this place?

Is it possible for Neil to sound better than he does on the porch, singing his song carelessly and quietly so we can learn it?

And when my friend Isaac drives up from Berkeley—my friend who I haven't seen in years, and who is now fifty-five, and whose mother has just died, and whose hair is whiter than ever—and he effortlessly shouts "I love you, Nic!" over his shoulder just before driving off, why do I not say it back? What, am I waiting for the next time I see him? Because, well, do I even want to ask? I mean, when will the next time be? And how many more will we get?

"I feel like I picked you up one month ago," Shannon says as he drives me to the airport, "but how long has it really been?"

"Um . . . nine days?"

"Crazy," he says, "right?" And then, "Are you feeling carsick?"

When was the last time I had a secret like this, a private sound in my headphones, a sound no one else has yet heard, and which I feel is so incredible it could just change the world? And though I know it's not going to change any world, except maybe my own, really, actually, doesn't it sound like it could? And is it enough that I'm wearing a hat and glasses and a mask and headphones?

Or can the people around me on this airplane all tell what I'm feeling? And why do I want to hide it from them anyway?

I keep listening, starting it over and listening again, and though most of these people are actually sleeping right now and so the windows are all shut and I can't see outside, I still know that I'm flying, even when I shut my eyes and listen closer, but where am I really? Am I in a place or above it? Am I the same person I was when I left on this trip? Am I becoming someone new or someone I was before? And do I want any peanuts? Or another club soda?

Later, when I'm at home, I say, Hey, can I send you some notes?

And Shannon says, "Yeah, whatcha got?"

OK, in the second verse, I say, when the vocals and drums come in, try muting the guitars—so that it's just drums and synth? And can we use the rototoms earlier? And do we really want the full two minutes of intro?

And even after I send him those notes, I keep listening and listening, and then when I'm playing the rough mixes for my daughter one day, she says, "Are people going to hear this?"

And I wonder, will they?

And will we play shows?

And if we do, where?

And actually, what is this? What am I even asking?

Is this a band?

Is this a new band?

Am I the drummer?

Or am I just a guy listening to music here, with my daughter inside my living room, still wondering if I'm in a place or above it? Like I'm sensing a whole life flying past? Knowing it's there, even if I can't see it? Thinking, there it all goes?

What do I want for dinner? I don't know, do you have any ideas? And hey, wait, Abby, will you listen to this? Isn't it great?

ACKNOWLEDGMENTS

Thank you, Daniel Wallace, Matthew Vollmer, Leslie Jamison, April Lawson, Shannon Ferguson, Rosecrans Baldwin, Darren Jessee, Nat Jacks, and Jack Shoemaker, all of whom helped this project take shape. The most love and gratitude goes to my family, Abby and Frances.

The following essays were published in slightly different forms in various magazines and anthologies. "In Tennis, Love Means Nothing," *The Morning News*; "An Eclipse," *Eclipse over Clemson*; and an excerpt from "The Fake ID" was first published in *Bring the Noise: The Best Pop Culture Essays from Barrelhouse Magazine*, under the title "Drumming."

Some names have been changed. The timeline might be a bit murky. I tried to get it all right.

© Abby Tripp

NIC BROWN is the author of the books *In Every Way*, *Doubles*, and *Floodmarkers*, which was selected as an Editors' Choice by *The New York Times Book Review*. He is the fiction editor of the *South Carolina Review*, and his writing has appeared in *The New York Times* and the *Harvard Review*, among many other publications. As a drummer, he has worked with Athenaeum, Ben Lee, Longwave, Skeleton Key, and Eszter Balint. A graduate of Columbia University and the Iowa Writers' Workshop, he has served as the Grisham Writer in Residence at the University of Mississippi and is now an associate professor of creative writing at Clemson University. Find out more at www.nicbrown.net.